UNDERSTANDING GOD'S MASTER PLAN

THE ANGEL ASSIGNMENT

REBECCA BRAND

Dedication

To Lynn Dawbin,

My only 'regret' in waiting for this book to be released is that you didn't get to hold a copy before you were promoted to Heaven. But now, you know far more than we ever could on this side of eternity… I'm looking forward to catching up with you someday.

THE ANGEL ASSIGNMENT

Copyright © 2025 Rebecca Brand

Paperback ISBN: 978-1-915223-49-4

All rights reserved.

No part of this publication may be reproduced, stored in a retrieval system, or transmitted in any form or by any means, electronic, mechanical, photocopying or otherwise, without the prior written consent of the publisher, except as provided by United Kingdom copyright law. Short extracts may be used for review purposes with credits given.

Main Bible Translation: ESV
Unless otherwise indicated, all Scripture quotations are from the ESV® Bible (The Holy Bible, English Standard Version®), © 2001 by Crossway, a publishing ministry of Good News Publishers. Used by permission. All rights reserved

Other Bible Translations:
Scripture quotations marked KJV are quotations from The Authorized (King James) Version. Rights in the Authorized Version in the United Kingdom are vested in the Crown. Reproduced by permission of the Crown's patentee, Cambridge University Press.

Scripture quotations marked NLT are taken from the Holy Bible, New Living Translation, copyright © 1996, 2004, 2015 by Tyndale House Foundation. Used by permission of Tyndale House Publishers, Inc., Carol Stream, Illinois 60188. All rights reserved.

Published by
Maurice Wylie Media
Your Inspirational & Christian Book Publisher

Publisher's statement: Throughout this book, the love for our God is such that whenever we refer to Him, we honour Him with capitals. On the other hand, when referring to the devil, we refuse to acknowledge him with any honour to the point of violating grammatical rules and withholding capitalisation.

Endorsements

"***The Angel Assignment*** is a powerful and uplifting book that helps us better understand the important role angels play in God's story and our lives today. With wisdom, clarity, and deep biblical insight, Rebecca shows how angels are part of God's redemptive plan to bring about His purposes on earth. This book clears up confusion, brings a fresh perspective, and keeps Christ at the centre of it all. It reminds us that we're not alone in the spiritual battle and encourages us to live with purpose, faith, and a greater awareness of heaven's involvement in our everyday lives as God's Master Plan heads towards fulfilment. A truly inspiring read for every believer."

Len Buttner, International Prophet & Founder of Eagle Ascend Ministries

"***The Angel Assignment*** is a gift to the body of Christ and a timely invitation for you to go deeper in your walk with God. Drawing from her own encounters and years of theological study, Rebecca writes with a reverence for Scripture, prophetic clarity, and a deep love for Jesus. She doesn't just talk about the supernatural—she lives it. This book is more than an exploration of angels; it is an invitation to see the unseen, to stand firm in spiritual battles, and to witness the ways God's purposes are accomplished within the world. Whether you are new to the subject or a seasoned believer, you will find your faith strengthened and your understanding of the topic of Angels deepened. Rebecca's voice is marked by compassion, strength, and unwavering devotion to God. I wholeheartedly recommend this book to anyone seeking to have a deeper understanding of the supernatural realm and a fuller awareness of God's presence and activity in our lives."

Lisa McKenzie, Founder of Hope and Joy Ministries

I know Rebecca as a passionate Jesus follower with a prophetic bent that motivates her to seek out and communicate life-giving truth to encourage and activate others in their faith. This book, initially prompted from her own experiences beginning in early childhood, unpacks biblical understanding on the topic of angels in accessible language. Rebecca has walked the journey of learning herself and weaves biblical teaching together with relatable stories and applications. I'm sure those who read this will learn something new and be enlightened with a greater understanding of their own role in the big and glorious plans of God.

Jill Smith, Prophet & Founder of Insight Ministries

Acknowledgements

First and foremost, I would like to express my gratitude to God, whose voice, grace, and guidance made this book possible. Without Him, none of this would exist.

To my husband, Kieren—your unwavering belief in me, your prayers, and your unconditional love gave me the courage to keep writing, even on the days I wanted to stop.

To our daughter, Sarai—you are my daily reminder of heaven's beauty.

To my friends and prayer warriors, your intercession and encouragement were vital through every stage of this journey.

And to those of you who are within the body of Christ who also feel socially awkward or simply that you don't belong, may this book honour your journey and inspire you to take your place in God's Master Plan, boldly.

Contents

Acknowledgements 9

Prologue 13

Introduction 15

Chapter 1   Before the Beginning 17

Chapter 2   Unveiling the Identity of Angels 31

Chapter 3   Understanding Divine Assignments 47

Chapter 4   Rebellion of satan 71

Chapter 5   Standing with Angels in Spiritual War 85

Chapter 6   Unveiling God's Eternal Master Plan 93

Notes 107

Contact 109

Prologue

I've often been asked when I first saw angels, and the truth is, I can't remember a time when I didn't. My first conversations with my mum about them came when I was around seven years old, from her recollection. Growing up in an atheistic household, I had no language at the time for what I saw except to call them my "fairy friends." Looking back, I realise that even at such a young age, I was witnessing something far more profound than childhood imaginings. What I didn't understand then, but I now see, is God's early invitation into the spiritual realm—a realm I would come to recognise as filled with angels and the demonic…always moving in ways that seemed "ordinary" to me but were extraordinary to everyone else. Yet, I couldn't articulate the difference between the natural and the supernatural in the early days, but all I knew was that angels were always around me, and I was never afraid when in their presence.

It wasn't until much later in life, during a season of deep personal struggle and spiritual growth, that I began to understand why I had been given the gift of seeing into the spiritual realm. It wasn't a curse, as I once thought, but a divine calling—one that would shape the trajectory of my life and ministry. When I encountered Jesus and embraced His saving grace, I began to understand that the angels weren't just protectors; they were also messengers and warriors, fulfilling roles that would one day align with the master plan God had set in motion for humanity.

Through the years, I came to learn that the spiritual realm is not something distant or disconnected from the world we live in. It is real. It is active. And, as I would discover in the pages of Scripture, angels are a key part of God's plan for us—a plan that continues to unfold, even now.

This book is an invitation into that realm. It is a glimpse into the world of angels and the spiritual battles that shape our lives, whether we see them or not. It is a journey of discovery, one that I've been on for decades. And it's a story of how, through the grace of God, I have come to understand my role as a prophetess, called to speak truth, to expose the works of darkness, and to share the revelations God has shown me about His heavenly messengers.

You may not see what I see, but I believe the time is coming when we will all come to understand the supernatural world in a much deeper way—through the eyes of faith, through the power of Scripture, and the guiding presence of the Holy Spirit. For, in the end, we are all part of a much larger story than we can imagine, and the angels are here to remind us of that eternal truth.

Introduction

It was just after God repeatedly highlighted the word **"angels"** to me as I was studying the Bible that I knew He desired to give me insight into them. I quickly learned that angels are mentioned over 300 times in Scripture and appear in 34 books of the Bible—more than half of them, to be precise. We also see numerous instances of angelic encounters with humanity throughout Scripture. Realising this, it has to be that God wants us to understand His truths regarding angels; otherwise, why would He make them so prominent in the Bible? Or why would He ensure that the canon of Scripture included them and take the time to outline their roles if we weren't meant to take note of these somewhat "mystical" beings?

Like many, I once held my own views on the role that angels play in the Kingdom of God. Some people exalt them, others dismiss their existence, and many remain uncertain or confused. I hope these pages will clarify their purpose within the Kingdom, the lives of believers, and the world.

We have a part to play in God's infinite plan, alongside the angels of God, who have stood in His presence. Therefore, to truly understand them, let's not be scared, intimidated, or even in awe of them, because it is God's perfect plan that we will co-exist together in eternity. It is there where our spirits will worship God forever, alongside the angels who have been doing so since before time began.

CHAPTER ONE

Before the Beginning

"There is a master plan. History is His story."

Rick Warren

(American Christian pastor and author)

From the beginning of time, God's plan has always included more than what we see with our natural eyes. As I studied Scripture and listened to the Holy Spirit, I began to realise something powerful: angels are not just side characters in biblical stories—they are essential participants in the unfolding of God's eternal design.

We often think of angels as messengers or guardians, which they are. But their purpose is much deeper—they are intricately woven into God's master plan for redemption, worship, and eternity. Understanding this shifts our focus from isolated encounters to a much broader vision of God's Kingdom.

In the Old Testament, God gave Moses detailed instructions for building the tabernacle. Every dimension, material, and design element reflected a heavenly reality. In fact, Hebrews 8:5 tells us:

"They serve a copy and shadow of the heavenly things."

This means God wasn't just giving Moses a building blueprint—He was revealing a divine pattern. One that reflects what exists in the heavenly realm, including the presence and role of angels.

In Revelation, we get a glimpse of that heavenly realm. We see angels worshipping, declaring God's holiness, executing judgement, and standing in awe before His throne. The continuity between the Old and New Testaments is striking—God has always included angelic beings in His work among us.

This is why angels aren't an "add-on" to the Christian faith. They are part of the divine order we are heading towards. When Jesus returns and establishes His Kingdom in fullness, we will reign with Him, and we will do so *alongside* the angels.

This isn't speculation. Hebrews 12:22 paints a vivid picture of the heavenly city:

> *"You have come to Mount Zion, to the city of the living God, the heavenly Jerusalem. You have come to thousands upon thousands of angels in joyful assembly…"*

We aren't just going to "visit" heaven—we're being prepared to live in harmony with God's divine hosts. Angels are not distant from our future; they are part of our eternal family.

I remember the first time I realised that angels weren't just part of Bible stories—they were part of *my* story, too. Not just as protectors but as co-labourers in the Kingdom, intimately involved in the divine plan unfolding over centuries. That revelation didn't come in a flash—it came slowly, as God opened my eyes through Scripture, prayer, and sometimes, quite literally.

Chapter 1 - Before the Beginning

But before we go too far, let's go back to the beginning. Or rather, before the beginning; before Adam walked in the Garden, or before the stars were flung into place, because there was a plan. Not a reactionary one. A *master plan*. God's design wasn't just to create a world—it was to create a family. A people who would dwell with Him, worship Him, and one day reign with Him.

And angels? They were there. They witnessed it. They shouted for joy when the foundations of the earth were laid.[1] They were part of that original design—not as equals with us, but as participants in God's glory, each with their appointed role.

Sometimes, when I think about the future—what eternity with God might look like—I don't imagine clouds or harps. I see the *Temple of the Living God*. I see Jesus dwelling among His people, angels in joyful assembly, and a redeemed humanity walking in step with heaven's rhythm.

This isn't fantasy. Scripture tells us clearly that it's all connected. The Old Testament tabernacle mirrored heaven. The throne room John saw in Revelation is filled with angels worshipping day and night. And here we are—invited into this story, preparing to live forever with God and His heavenly hosts.

Yet, this master plan or story has two parts. The first part is the ministry angels have with humanity and our being with the LORD in heaven, which I will go through in this chapter, and the second part is God's reason for everything, which I will discuss in a later chapter.

To begin unpacking this divine narrative, we'll first explore the crucial role angels play in ministering to humanity and what our future with the LORD in heaven looks like—a journey that not only reveals their significance but also sets the stage for understanding the deeper reasons behind God's grand design.

---

[1] Job 38:7.

With this in mind, have you ever noticed that there are fascinating accounts of angel encounters or even demonic forces at work that we can read about? Rest assured, as we will see throughout this book, it is not a case of whether angels and demons are real (they very much are) but more about us understanding why God has them in *His master plan*.

Now, we know that angels are not omnipotent (which means they do not have unlimited power because they are limited to the power and authority God grants them). They are also not omnipresent (which means that they cannot always be everywhere, like God). We can see this when Daniel was waiting for his prayer to be answered, yet the angel with his message was stuck in warfare. So, angels can only be in one place at a time. This reiterates that they are not God, because they have been created.

We also know that because angels are spiritual, they are mainly invisible to the human eye. However, as we have already heard, they will manifest into a masculine form, or we may encounter angels within our dreams and visions.

One striking example of this is found in the life of Jacob. Known as a dreamer, he repeatedly encountered angels in his prophetic dreams, as recorded in Genesis 28 and 31. Yet, this man was a con artist, a liar, and a manipulator—his very name, Jacob, means "deceiver." He stole the birthright from his brother Esau, and Jacob even lied to his father, Isaac, on his deathbed, when Isaac was almost blind, to receive his father's blessing. So, you can understand Esau's anger towards his brother at the time.

However, God looked out for Jacob because he was the "line of promise." The twelve tribes of Israel were to come from his lineage, and we can read how God sent an army of angels to meet with him in Genesis:

> *"And Jacob went on his way, and the angels of God met him. And when Jacob saw them, he said, This is God's host: and he called the name of that place* **Mahanaim***."* Genesis 32:1-2

The word Mahanaim is taken from Hebrew, meaning (mahănayim) "two tents" or "two armies," meaning Jacob's family. This was when he was about to meet up with his brother, Esau, again, and the other army was the angels.

Strangely, this place is also where Jacob wrestled with God. Although, again, many believe this was Jesus pre-incarnate. We later read in Chapter 32 that an angelic stranger visited Jacob at night. They wrestled throughout the night until daybreak, at which point the stranger crippled Jacob with a blow to his hip that disabled him with a limp for the rest of his life. It was then that Jacob realised what had happened:

> *"I saw God face to face, and yet my life was spared."*
> Genesis 32:30

In the process, Jacob, the deceiver, receives a new name—Israel, which means, *"He struggles with God."* We can learn so much from this struggle because we also read that God blessed Jacob as in Genesis 32:29. In the end, Jacob does what we all must do… he confronts his failures, weaknesses, sins, and everything hurting him, and faces God.

Scripture says that Jacob wrestled with God all night. Therefore, as we can imagine, it was an exhausting struggle that left him crippled. It was only after he came to grips with God and ceased his battle that he realised that he could not go on without God; from that, he received God's blessing.

Now, although this was a brief digression from angels themselves, the point is that this story saw Jacob wrestle with an angel in human form, and many angels surrounded him—yet I couldn't pass up a good learning opportunity for us all!

Abraham is another important character who has angels involved in his life during essential events. Two angels with the Lord appeared to him in Genesis 18. Those same two angels then appeared to Lot before destroying Sodom in Genesis 19. The angel of the LORD also prevented Abraham from sacrificing Isaac in Genesis 22. Lastly, Abraham was so trusting in the LORD that he was confident that an angel would guide his servant in finding a wife for Isaac in Genesis 24.

Think of Moses. For 80 years, God prepared him in the palace and then in the wilderness, before one day, he witnessed a burning bush that wasn't being consumed. There is nothing in Scripture to state that until this point, Moses had seen an angel,[2] but here, the angel of the LORD appeared to him from within the bush. I mean, how cool is this? Moses encountered an angel that day and heard from Yahweh when He identified Himself as the *"God of Abraham, Isaac and Jacob."* This was the day God commissioned Moses to lead His people out of Egypt.

So we can see from these few people that God not only uses angels to redirect our lives but also to make His will known in our lives and to communicate His decisions to people.

People in Scripture have also witnessed angels in their natural form, which, for instance, Daniel states in Chapter 10:

> *"I looked up and there before me was a man dressed in linen, with a belt of fine gold from Uphaz around his waist. His body was like topaz, his face like lightning, his eyes like flaming torches, his arms and legs*

---

[2] Exodus 3:2-4.

like the gleam of burnished bronze, and his voice like the sound of a multitude." Daniel 10:5-6

Like many people, Daniel trembled in this unnamed angel's presence. So, angels can communicate with us in various forms or ways.

Let's look quickly at the New Testament. Again, I am only going to scratch the surface because more than twenty interactions humans have experienced with angels are listed both in the Gospel accounts and in the rest of the New Testament.[a]

The first couple of interactions we talked about in the first chapter, but in the New Testament, angels appear to Zachariah in Jerusalem's temple, where he is told his wife Elizabeth will bear a son named John, who later became John the Baptist, as told by Luke 1:11-20.

Then, Gabriel was sent to the virgin Mary to inform her that she would miraculously conceive of our Saviour, who was to be named Jesus, as explained by Luke 1:26-38.

Amazingly, Joseph (Mary's fiancé) receives at least three separate visits from angels, mostly in dreams, where they instruct him on his fiancée and unborn child. Interestingly, it didn't matter whether the angel was in human or angelic form within the dream, because people like Jacob and Joseph knew they were angels.

The most famous account is when an angel announces to Bethlehem's shepherds[3] that Jesus had been born, and it was recorded that many angels also praised God for the unique miracle of Christ's birth to a virgin, which many of us sing about at Christmas.

From this point within Scripture and history, angels were then to minister to us regarding God's message, and establish the Gospel's message to humanity. There are so many accounts of this, but the last

---

[3] Luke 2:9-15.

one I want to focus on is that angels are also called to care for us, and the New Testament records a group of angels ministering to Jesus after His temptation by the devil:

> *"Then the devil left him, and angels came and attended him."* Matthew 4:11

This happened immediately before Jesus' ministry started. Angels also helped Elijah in the wilderness (Old Testament), so the angels are called to protect and deliver us in many ways.

One of my favourite Scriptures regarding angels is from 2 Kings 14-17, where it says:

> *"Then he sent horses and chariots and a strong force there. They went by night and surrounded the city. When the servant of the man of God got up and went out early the next morning, an army with horses and chariots had surrounded the city. "Oh no, my lord! What shall we do?" the servant asked. "Don't be afraid," the prophet answered. "Those who are with us are more than those who are with them." And Elisha prayed, "Open his eyes, Lord, so that he may see." Then the Lord opened the servant's eyes, and he looked and saw the hills full of horses and chariots of fire all around Elisha."*

This is where the King of Syria sent his army to Dothan after learning that Elisha was there. Yet, I love that Elisha replies to his helper, *"Don't be afraid…those who are with us are more than those who are with them."*

Do we truly realise this? Do we understand that God's army, which is fighting for us, consists of countless angels beyond our comprehension?

So many battles in our lives would be conquered if we could grasp God's promise that His angels were always nearby, ready to help us, but we seem to forget to invite God into our lives and circumstances.

Before we consider the "end times" regarding angels and humanity, I want us to understand that every believer should be encouraged because angels watch us and protect the Lord's interests.

Paul wrote in 1 Corinthians 4:9:

> *"We have been made a spectacle to the whole universe, to angels as well as to human beings."*

In other words, being a spectacle meant that the apostles were on "display" or "being watched." We see an account of the angels protecting God's interest when the angel of the LORD appeared to Hagar in the wilderness, as Genesis 16:7-14 explains. God sent them to minister to Hagar when she was pregnant with Ishmael (his name means "God hears"). The angel ensured that God's will for her life came to pass by prophesying to her about what her son would become.

Yet, often, angels work in unseen ways because it doesn't serve God's purpose for us to perceive angels within our lives. This is because a large number of people still glorify angels, and I believe this is probably why God chooses to conceal them. If men like Daniel tremble[4] and men like the Apostle John worship them,[5] then, honestly, how much more likely are we going to respond incorrectly if they manifested before us?

God, therefore, will only open our eyes to see angels when it serves His purpose for our lives.

And so, this leads us to understand that all of this is only God's temporary plan, and although there are some things that angels

---

[4] Daniel 10:8. [5] Revelation 19:10.

and humans have in common, many things separate us. Though sin entered both the angelic and human spheres, only the sin of humans can and will be forgiven. Christ came to die for the sins of humanity, not of angels.

However, when it comes to hierarchy, angels rank higher than humanity. This is simply because, in God's order, the hierarchy of angels has to do with their proximity to humanity, who sin, and thus, how close a being then currently stands to Him. I will explain the hierarchy of angels in the next chapter, but for now, let me explain why angels currently "rank" higher than humanity.

In the first chapter of Hebrews, we are told that Jesus was above the angels since He was and is God:

> *"The Son radiates God's own glory and expresses the very character of God, and he sustains everything by the mighty power of his command. When he had cleansed us from our sins, he sat down in the place of honour at the right hand of the majestic God in heaven. This shows that the Son is far greater than the angels, just as the name God gave him is greater than their names."*
> Hebrews 1:3-4

Now let's look at Hebrews 2:7-9:

> *"Yet for a little while you made them a little lower than the angels and crowned them with glory and honour. You gave them authority over all things." Now when it says "all things," it means nothing is left out. But we have not yet seen all things put under their authority. What we do see is Jesus, who for a little while was given a position "a little lower than the angels"; and because he suffered death for us, he is now "crowned with glory and honour." Yes, by God's grace, Jesus tasted death for everyone."*

In other words, when Jesus became a man, He was made lower than the angels in the sense that He took on human flesh. He was still God. He was God in human flesh, but He was temporarily lower than the angels because He took on our form. Therefore, Hebrews 2:7-9 implies that humans are made lower than the angels because of their sinful nature that arises from Adam and Eve.

This is why it is essential to note what Scripture says: those people who try to command the angels to do whatever they are demanding or decreeing in their prayers, rather than seeking God's will for those circumstances, have things in the wrong order. Angels will never take orders from us because they rank higher; only God directs them as He sees fit.

Scripture also never says that we are equal to the angels—it only reveals that we are lower than them while we live here. This is because, as God's children, we will be given a higher position than the angels. After all, we're not only created in God's image, but redeemed by Christ.[6]

Yet, for those of us who go to heaven, Scripture shows that someday we will then judge angels. The following Scripture from 1 Corinthians is in Paul's letter to the church in Corinth, but the apostle Paul tells us that believers will not only judge the world but also judge angels:

> *"Don't you realise that we will judge angels? So you should surely be able to resolve ordinary disputes in this life."*
> 1 Corinthians 6:3

Here, Paul is saying: if we can't get our lives in order, how will we fulfil what God has planned for us in the coming days?

We know that Scripture teaches us that God will judge the fallen angels from Isaiah 24:21-22, 2 Peter 2:4, Jude 1:6, and Revelation 21:10. But what does Paul mean when he says we will also judge angels?

---

[6] Galatians 3:13.

The passage is surprising because Paul assumes his readers already know their role in the final judgement. He asks rhetorical questions twice, "Do you not know?" And yet, if it weren't for this passage, how many Christians *would* know today what is to happen?

As jarring as it may sound, Paul likely has in mind an active, delegated role for believers in the final judgement. Now, this interpretation is widely accepted in church history, and it does have biblical support.[b]

One of the clearest Old Testament references to believers' role in the final judgement is found in Daniel's vision of the Son of Man:

> *"And judgment was given for the saints of the Most High, and the time came when the saints possessed the kingdom."* Daniel 7:22

In the New Testament, Jesus speaks of a role for His disciples (Jesus Followers) in judging Israel:

> *"Truly, I say to you, in the new world, when the Son of Man will sit on his glorious throne, you who have followed me will also sit on twelve thrones, judging the twelve tribes of Israel."* Matthew 19:28

Further, in the parable of the talents, found in the Book of Matthew, Jesus alludes to degrees of authority granted to believers on the day of Judgement:

> *"His master said to him, 'Well done, good and faithful servant. You have been faithful over a little; I will set you over much"* Matthew 25:21

Chapter 1 - Before the Beginning

Now, you can read these passages and think, well, it doesn't explicitly say that we will be ruling over angels. But bear with me because God had temporarily allotted jurisdiction of the pagan nations to a ruling class of angels, known as the "sons of God" in the Old Testament. We can find this in Deuteronomy:

> *"When the Most High gave to the nations their inheritance, when he divided mankind, he fixed the borders of the peoples according to the number of the sons of God."* Deuteronomy 32:8

In other words, throughout Scripture and history, angels have worked to carry out God's judgements, directing the destinies of nations that disobeyed God. Then, God pronounces condemnation on these angels because of their unjust rule:

> *"I said, 'You are gods, sons of the Most High, all of you; nevertheless, like men you shall die, and fall like any prince.'"* Psalm 82:6-7

Part of God's redemptive plan (as we know) is to overthrow these demonic kingdoms and replace them with the Kingdom of his Son, with believers ruling as co-heirs.

> *"Except to hold on to what you have until I come.' To the one who is victorious and does my will to the end, I will give authority over the nations— that one 'will rule them with an iron sceptre and will dash them to pieces like pottery'—just as I have received authority from my Father. I will also give that one the morning star."* Revelation 2:25-28

This passage right here gives us a glimpse of God's master plan.

Angels, until Jesus returns, will help humanity to fulfil God's plan for their lives, and then, those of us who are victorious and ascend, will rule over the nations and the morning star, which, in another chapter, I discuss further. But in case you don't know who the morning star is… it's the angels.

So, my question for us now is, why study angels?

Because they're part of the eternal reality God is calling us into. They're not mystical extras; they are messengers, warriors, worshippers—part of the Kingdom we're destined for.

So, let's begin at the foundation. If we're going to understand angels' purposes, we first need to understand **who they are,** because when I set out to write this book, I wanted to include the role that angels play in what is to come and what will happen when we get to eternity. This, after all, is God's master plan, and we need to understand our roles in His plan because physical death is only the beginning for Christians.

CHAPTER TWO

Unveiling the Identity of Angels

"While we do not place our faith directly in angels, we should place it in the God who rules the angels; then we can have peace."

Billy Graham

I pray that people come to understand just how important angels are to God. However, with so much misinformation about angels circulating in books, on the internet, and across social media, we must turn to Scripture, for God's Word is truth.[7] When it comes to this subject, the Bible is crystal clear about two key points—both of which we must apply to our lives if we are not already doing so.

I often joke that if I had a dollar for every time these two points were incorrectly spoken about in the church, I'd be rich! But in reality, it saddens me because, as mentioned, Scripture is not vague on this matter, and so, the fact is the church is not clear on what Scripture speaks on these two points. When it comes to the topic of angels, I believe the church is still **"drinking milk"** instead of "**eating solid food**."[8] The reality of spiritual warfare and the spiritual realm needs to be openly discussed. Yet, the church often either remains silent or speaks based on misconceptions, and unfortunately, many get it wrong.

---

[7] Psalm 119:160. [8] Hebrews 5:13.

We need confidence in God's role for us and a clear understanding of what He says about angels. This is why I believe this topic must be taught in the Church today, and we need to understand the following key points as a foundation when talking about angels. So, what are these points?

1. We Are NEVER to Worship Angels

> *"Do not let anyone who delights in false humility and the worship of angels disqualify you. Such a person also goes into great detail about what they have seen; they are puffed up with idle notions by their unspiritual mind."* Colossians 2:18

2. We Should NOT Pray to Angels

> *"I, John, am the one who heard and saw these things. And when I had heard and seen them, I fell down to worship at the feet of the angel who had been showing them to me. But he said to me, "Don't do that! I am a fellow servant with you and with your fellow prophets and with all who keep the words of this scroll. Worship God!"*
> Revelation 22:8-9

This second point is especially concerning because, although no verse explicitly says, *"You shall not pray to angels,"* Scripture makes it abundantly clear that we are not to do so. Why? Because **prayer is an act of worship**, and as we just read in Revelation, angels reject our worship. If they reject our worship, they also reject our prayers, because offering prayer or worship to anyone other than God is **idolatry**.

Yet, how often do we hear people—even pastors—praying for an angel's protection? Every time I hear it, I cringe inside. We should be praying to **God alone**, who, in His perfect will, determines whether He will send His angels to assist us.

There is no **wiggle room** in these two points. **Angels were created by God**.[9] Like us, they are spiritual beings, though some also have a bodily form. However, as created beings, they are **never** to replace God in our lives.

This is why I believe **Scripture provides limited details** on the nature and origin of angels. Too much focus on them could distract from the Bible's central theme—**God's salvation for humanity**.

What we do know is this:

> *"By the word of the LORD the heavens were made, their starry host by the breath of His mouth."* Psalm 33:6

While the Bible doesn't specify exactly when God created the angels, we do know that it was before the world was formed. Genesis 2 confirms this, and Job 38 reveals that angels were present, worshipping God, as He laid the foundations of the earth:

> *"Where were you when I laid the earth's foundation? Tell me, if you understand. Who marked off its dimensions? Surely you know! Who stretched a measuring line across it? On what were its footings set, or who laid its cornerstone—while the morning stars sang together, and all the angels shouted for joy?"* Job 38:4-7

Only God knows the exact timeline of creation. However, this passage clearly shows that angels existed when the earth was formed.

It's also important to remember that because **God exists outside of time and space**, much of what He did before the foundation of the world remains beyond human understanding. These events took place **outside of time as we know it**, and we must trust in His divine order rather than speculate beyond what Scripture reveals.

---

[9] Genesis 2:1.

And finally, before we get into who the angels are, I think I need to mention that we need to be careful not to "add" to Scripture. God's canon has sixty-six books, so it doesn't need "new revelations" being added about angels.

Distinguishing Scripture from Historical Texts

The term *canon* refers to the collection of books recognised as divinely inspired and, therefore, included in the Bible as we know it, determined through God's direction. The formation of the biblical canon wasn't a single event; rather, it was affirmed multiple times throughout history. Between the Council of Rome (382 AD) and the Council of Trent (1546 AD), the Church consistently reaffirmed the same 73 books—46 in the Old Testament and 27 in the New Testament—as the authoritative canon of the Christian Bible.

With this in mind, we must be cautious when reading books about angels that fall outside this canon. For example, books like *Maccabees* and *Tobias* are included in the Catholic Bible but not in the Protestant Bible. Then, there are texts like *Enoch*, discovered among the Dead Sea Scrolls. While these writings are historically significant and can provide valuable cultural and theological insights, they should be read as informative or historical references rather than as divinely inspired Scripture.

Although these texts may offer deeper context for understanding certain biblical themes, they should never distract us from or override the authority of God's Word as revealed in the Bible.

I have seen what happens when people read books like Enoch and become fascinated with the other archangels not mentioned in canonical Scripture. Yet, we need to recognise that the world has created an idol with the demonic, angelic, and spiritual realms, and therefore, we need to trust what God has given us—as His truth—for the Church.

I have said a lot about being "careful," but this simply means that we need to walk in Spiritual Truth by discerning what God intended for us.

I believe God has given us hundreds of Scriptures regarding angels for a reason; after all, Scripture is to help us understand who God ultimately is. It is with this in mind that I want to look at the angels mentioned explicitly in Scripture.

Interestingly, the term "angel" comes from the Greek word *angelos,* and the Hebrew equivalent is *malak*. Both words mean "messenger", and yet, out of the hundreds of angelic references, only four angels have actual names that have been shared with us, and even then, one of those names is more implied. Only two of these angels are working for God to advance His master plan.

1. Gabriel

Gabriel appears in four passages of Scripture, but with each encounter, he comes with a message and mentions Jesus in different ways. This is why most people assume he is an archangel, but this is never stated within Scripture.

Let us look at these Scriptures.

He appears to the prophet Daniel in the Old Testament (Daniel 8:16, 9:22), where, the first time he speaks with Daniel, Gabriel explains that the King in his vision will destroy many people and take His stand against the prince of princes (Daniel 8:25). Now, understandably, Daniel is upset by this. So, he prays to God for mercy, and once again, God sends Gabriel to Daniel, but this time, Gabriel tells Daniel that the Messiah (ruler) will be put to death (9:25-26). That probably wasn't what Daniel was hoping to hear from God!

> *"And I heard a man's voice between the banks of the Ulai, who called, and said, 'Gabriel, make this man understand the vision."* Daniel 8:16
>
> *"And he informed me, and talked with me, and said, "O Daniel, I have now come forth to give you skill to understand."* Daniel 9:22
>
> *"Know therefore and understand, that from the going forth of the command to restore and build Jerusalem until Messiah the Prince, there shall be seven weeks and sixty-two weeks; The street shall be built again, and the wall, even in troublesome times. And after the sixty-two weeks Messiah shall be cut off, but not for Himself; And the people of the prince who is to come shall destroy the city and the sanctuary. The end of it shall be with a flood, and till the end of the war desolations are determined."* Daniel 9:25-56

Then, looking at the New Testament, Gabriel next appears to the priest Zechariah, who was to become the father of John the Baptist.[10] I find this an incredible part in Scripture because this was when the Israelites had just experienced 400 years of silence from God. After all, the last time God spoke to them was through the prophet Malachi. Therefore, at this point, God sends an angel with a message to Zechariah.

> *"And the angel answered him, "I am Gabriel. I stand in the presence of God, and I was sent to speak to you and to bring you this good news."* Luke 1:19

When Gabriel tells Zechariah that he will have a baby boy in his old age, and his son will be the one who would go before the Lord *"in the spirit and power of Elijah…to make ready a people prepared for the Lord"*—Luke 1:17, you would think that Zechariah would have praised God for the

---

[10] Luke 1:19.

message of hope and grace. Yet, as a temple priest who is a law-abiding man, married, and old (like Abraham when told he would conceive)[11] Zechariah doesn't rise in faith and accept the prophecy.

Nope…instead…he questions Gabriel in disbelief about the chances of him conceiving a child at his age.

Lastly, Gabriel appears to Mary, the mother of Jesus.[12] This is such a contrast to Zechariah because, in the natural, Mary appears to have far less going for her. For instance, at that time, she was a young woman who also held no titles or positions within the local community and had no husband either (although she was engaged). Yet, God still wanted to bless humanity through this virgin.

> *"In the sixth month the angel Gabriel was sent from God to a city of Galilee named Nazareth…"* Luke 1:26

Yet, in all of these different passages, we learn some amazing things about Gabriel himself because, yes, he is an angel who appears in human form.[13] Yet, Gabriel doesn't seem to just come off as your average "man" in appearance, because when Gabriel shows up…basically…his appearance somewhat frightens people.

> *"The man Gabriel, whom I had seen in the vision at the first, came to me in swift flight at the time of the evening sacrifice."* Daniel 9:21

For example, when Gabriel first approaches Daniel, Scripture tells us that he is terrified. Daniel falls on his face at the sight of the angel.[14] Also, Daniel is sick for days after Gabriel's visit and the vision he brought.[15] Zechariah was equally "startled and gripped with fear,"[16] but to be fair to Zechariah, Gabriel did show up unannounced in what was supposed to be an empty temple. He was shocked by Gabriel's sudden appearance before him.

---

[11] Genesis 15:1-20. [12] Luke 1:26. [13] Daniel 9:21. [14] Daniel 8:17. [15] Daniel 8:27. [16] Luke 1:12.

> *"So he came near where I stood. And when he came, I was frightened and fell on my face. But he said to me, "Understand, O son of man, that the vision is for the time of the end."* Daniel 8:17

> *"And I, Daniel, was overcome and lay sick for some days. Then I rose and went about the king's business, but I was appalled by the vision and did not understand it."* Daniel 8:27

Incredibly, though, Gabriel also admits to standing in the very presence of God,[17] who sent him to Daniel, Zechariah, and Mary. God had asked this of Gabriel because he was selected to "deliver" critical messages of God's particular love and favour to these individuals, who had been chosen to be a part of God's plan for mankind.

> *"And there appeared to him an angel of the Lord standing on the right side of the altar of incense."* Luke 1:11

It is also suggested within Scripture that Gabriel had wings, because when Gabriel visited Daniel a second time, he came to him "in swift flight at the time of the evening sacrifice."[18] However, although "flight" might suggest wings, we need to be careful not to say this, as wings are not mentioned specifically.

2. Michael

Michael also appears in four passages of Scripture. However, he is the only angel to be described as an archangel within the canon of Scripture, as we see in the following:

> *"But even the archangel Michael, when he was disputing with the devil about the body of Moses, did not himself dare to condemn him for slander but said, 'The Lord rebuke you!'"* Jude 1:9

---

[17] Luke 1:11.   [18] Daniel 9:21.

Michael is the archangel who engages in spiritual warfare:

> *"Then war broke out in heaven. Michael and his angels fought against the dragon, and the dragon and his angels fought back."* Revelation 12:7

Michael is also referred to as a Chief Prince who works to protect God's people in Daniel Chapter 10. This is where people read the Book of Enoch and assume that, because the following Scripture states "one of the chief princes," it means that there are other archangels or chief princes because Enoch talks about them by name. Yet, it does not state their names within our canon, so again, we must be 'careful' not to add them to Scripture. Yet, this verse is where Michael is spoken of by another angel, one who is not named, and this angel talks of coming to Daniel sooner, but he is delayed.

> *"Michael, one of the chief princes, came to help me, because I was detained there with the king of Persia."* Daniel 10:13

In the next chapter, we will discuss the different types of angels and why the Scripture found in Daniel 10 shows that many scholars, including the late Billy Graham, and even I, believe that angels have a hierarchical system (i.e., they have different roles to play within God's Kingdom).

3. lucifer

Many people misunderstand who lucifer truly is, often picturing him as some equal opposite of God, which is far from biblical truth. Lucifer was originally a high-ranking angel, full of beauty, wisdom, and purpose. He was created by God, not as evil, but as glorious. Yet pride entered his heart, and he rebelled against the very One who made him. In doing so, he fell from his position in heaven and became satan, the adversary. To grasp the reality of spiritual warfare and deception today, we must first understand this core truth: He is not a god, not an equal force of darkness, but a *fallen angel*—a created being who turned away from his Creator and now works in opposition to God's plan. Now, with this in mind, many will know this angel by many names. However, before his pride got in the way, his name was Hêlēl in Hebrew or lucifer in Greek, meaning "shining one or morning star." To fully grasp the nature of satan, we must recognise the many names and titles that Scripture uses to describe him. Each name reveals a different aspect of his character, tactics, and influence. Far from being a mere symbol of evil, satan is a real spiritual being who operates under various deceptive identities. These names not only expose who he is but also remind us of the nature of the battle we face.

The devil

The name devil comes from the Greek word *diabolos*, meaning "slanderer" or "accuser." But satan is the one who accuses God's people, aiming to shame and condemn them before the Lord.

> *"The great dragon was hurled down—that ancient serpent called the devil, or Satan, who leads the whole world astray..."* Revelation 12:9

> *"Then Jesus was led by the Spirit into the wilderness to be tempted by the devil."* Matthew 4:1

beelzebub

Also rendered beelzebul, this name means "lord of the flies" or "lord of dung", and it was used by the Pharisees to refer to the prince of demons. They accused Jesus of casting out demons by the power of beelzebub—linking him directly to satan.

> *"It is only by Beelzebul, the prince of demons, that this fellow drives out demons."* Matthew 12:24

> *"By Beelzebul, the prince of demons, he is driving out demons."* Luke 11:15

A Liar

One of satan's most destructive weapons is deceit. Jesus describes him as the *"father of lies,"* the one who twists truth to enslave hearts and minds.

> *"When he lies, he speaks his native language, for he is a liar and the father of lies."* John 8:44

A Thief

He is also described as a thief—one who steals joy, purpose, identity, and even life. His mission is to destroy everything God intends for good.

> *"The thief comes only to steal and kill and destroy; I have come that they may have life, and have it to the full."* John 10:10

Yet, even with these names, most people will know him as satan. So, what else can we learn from Scripture? As mentioned above, it shows us he is a fallen angel:

> *"How you are fallen from heaven, O shining star, son of the morning! You have been thrown down to the earth, you who destroyed the nations of the world."* Isaiah 14:12

Now, some of you might be thinking, well, that Scripture doesn't mention angels, only stars. However, the Biblical authors, along with all the people at the time, would have understood what was meant by this text, and we need to remember that these books were written for the Israelites. So, with that said, the ancient Israelites and all ancient cultures thought of the stars as divine beings, so they saw them as heavenly creatures that were glorious, shining bright, and high above. Therefore, stars symbolised created beings who were with God in Heaven, serving Him and His purposes.[c]

Remember that satan was thrown out of Heaven for rebelling against his Creator, God. But before this, Scripture gives us another description of him and shows us that he was a beautiful, wise guardian cherub in the Garden of Eden. Again, as mentioned, I will go into the types of angels in the next chapter, but Ezekiel gives us a glimpse of satan. I just need to note that the first person spoken of in Ezekiel 28 is very clearly human, being the *King of Tyre,* also reiterates this by saying:

> *"Yet you **are** a man, a lucifer and not a God."* Ezekiel 28:2

However, in the second part of this passage, we get a picture of lucifer. Some Bible interpreters believe this part of the passage is an allegory of satan's fall because no mere human could claim to be in Eden or an anointed cherub! Others refer to this as a "dual prophecy"—comparing the pride of the King of Tyre to the pride of satan:

> *"This is what the Sovereign Lord says: "You were the seal of perfection, full of wisdom and perfect in beauty. You were in Eden, the garden of God; …Your settings and mountings were made of gold; on the day you were created, they were prepared. You were anointed as a guardian cherub, for so I ordained you. You were on the holy mount of God… You were blameless in your ways from the day you were created*

till wickedness was found in you. Your heart became proud on account of your beauty, and you corrupted your wisdom because of your splendour. So, I threw you to the earth."
Ezekiel 28:12-19

And so, here on earth, lucifer has been given *temporary reign* as the prince of the power, or more simply, the prince of this world, along with all the other fallen angels.

"Judgment will come because the ruler of this world has already been judged." John 16:11

We know that satan has control of this world[19] and that he masquerades as an angel of light.[20] But as Christians, we know that he is literally leading the whole world astray.[21] Ultimately, he is a thief,[22] a murderer, and the father of lies,[23] because he spoke the very first lie to Adam and Eve in the Garden of Eden,[24] saying:

"You surely will not die."

Which brought death to us all.[25] Yet, we know (and need to remember) that his time is short because *he has been judged*[26] because of his pride. Upon Christ's return, satan and his minions will be thrown into the eternal fire after the Millennial reign,[27] which leads to his destruction.

4. Abaddon (Apollyon)

And so, we come to the last angel who is named in Scripture, and his name is Ăbaddōn in Hebrew or Apollúon in Greek. This angel isn't a barrel of laughs because in Hebrew, his name "Abaddon" means "place of destruction", and in Greek, "Apollyon" literally means "The Destroyer." So you get the picture of what his role is. I will call this angel Abaddon from here on.

---

[19] 2 Corinthians 4:4.
[20] 2 Corinthian 11:14.
[21] Revelation 12:9.
[22] John 10:10.
[23] John 8:44.
[24] Genesis 3:4.
[25] Romans 5:12.
[26] John 16:11.
[27] Revelation 20:10.

Now, in Revelation Chapters 8-9, John describes a period during the end times when angels sound seven trumpets. Each trumpet signals the coming of a new judgement on the people of Earth.

> *"And the fifth angel blew his trumpet, and I saw a star fallen from heaven to earth, and he was given the key to the shaft of the bottomless pit. Then from the smoke came locusts on the earth, and they were given power like the power of scorpions of the earth. They had as king over them the angel of the Abyss, whose name in Hebrew is Abaddon and in Greek is Apollyon that is, Destroyer."* Revelation 9:1-3,11

So, when the fifth angel blows his trumpet, the Abyss, which is a great smoking pit, will open, and a horde of demonic "locusts" will rise out of it—sounds great, right? But the sad thing is how many people think hell will be fun. I remember, as an atheist, saying openly that "hell is where the party will be"… oh, how blinded I was to the truth back then because these demonic creatures will be given the power to torture any person who does not bear God's seal. And the pain they inflict will be so intense that sufferers will wish to die. So, Abaddon is the ruler of the Abyss and the king of these demonic locusts.

Just a side note—some people think that Abaddon is often used as another name for satan. However, this is incorrect, because Scripture seems to distinguish the two. We find satan later in Revelation when he is imprisoned for 1,000 years (millennial reign), but he is released to wreak havoc on the earth and ultimately receives his final, eternal punishment. However, whatever Abaddon's role is currently, he is an instrument of judgement that God will use during the End Times, so there is some debate about where his allegiance falls.

A Name Implied — The Angel of the LORD

There are quite a few instances within Scripture where an angel is called "the Angel of the Lord," but upon closer inspection, we will see that sometimes the Angel of the Lord is stated to be God Himself—Yahweh—where He appears in human form in the Old Testament.

In Genesis 16:7-13, we can see that this angel is no mere angel when He says:

"I will give you many descendants."

To which Hagar replies:

"You are the God who sees me."

Also, in Exodus 3:2-6, we see verses like this:

"There the angel of the Lord appeared to him in flames of fire from within a bush. "Do not come any closer," God said. "Take off your sandals, for the place where you are standing is holy ground." Then he said, "I am the God of your father, the God of Abraham, the God of Isaac and the God of Jacob." At this, Moses hid his face, because he was afraid to look at God." Exodus 3:2-6

The Bible Project[d] explains this well, but basically, the stories of Hagar, Moses, and others like it are inviting us into a kind of paradox—that Yahweh is, above all, inaccessible to us. But sometimes He reveals Himself to us in ways that we can see and understand; thus, this is where the Angel of the Lord shows up, because He is the Royal Glory of Yahweh, appearing as a human. In other words, the angel is distinct from God, but also IS God—sound familiar?

I believe this angel is Jesus because the Angel of the Lord's appearance ceased after Christ's incarnation. Some may disagree with that statement, but angels are mentioned numerous times in the New Testament; however, the Angel of the Lord is never mentioned after Christ's birth. We must understand that this is one of those "grey areas" as it is not explicitly told to us, but John says that God's word:

> *"Became human and set up a tabernacle among us."* John 1:14

Becoming a kind of "temple presence" of the invisible God (which is God's ultimate plan, and I'll speak of this in the final chapter to explain more), but if you remember Jesus in Mark 9:2-9 (along with the other Gospels), He took three of His followers up a mountain and His true identity was revealed at the Transfiguration. So, in essence, the angel of the Lord was God, who appeared to be human. And Jesus, who is God, now became a human.

Jesus reiterates this by declaring Himself to exist before Abraham:

> *"Very truly I tell you,"* Jesus answered, *"before Abraham was born, I am!"* John 8:58

This is why, in the New Testament, no one ever uses the phrase "Angel of the Lord" to describe Jesus. They wanted to avoid the idea that Jesus was merely an angel; for them, Jesus was Yahweh—God becoming human.

CHAPTER THREE
Understanding Divine Assignments

"There are nine orders of angels, to wit, angels, archangels, virtues, powers, principalities, dominations, thrones, cherubim, and seraphim."

Billy Graham

As mentioned, around 300 Scriptures mention angels. So if we think about it, I believe God wants us to pay attention to what is said about them. It's kind of logical.

So, this next topic is one of my favourite things to "speak" on, and (ultimately) why I felt I needed to write this book—being the different *types* of angels. We cannot study the subject of angels in Scripture without becoming aware of their ranks among the angels. Billy Graham said that the "evidence shows they are organised in terms of authority and glory."[e]

The difficulty in this, though, is that the Bible doesn't specifically identify a hierarchy of angels. Yet the Bible shows that there are different kinds of them. Scripture tells us that God controls His heavenly hosts,[28] and a few Scriptures "insinuate" some angels' position.

> *"I made the earth and created man on it; it was my hands that stretched out the heavens, and I commanded all their host."*
> Isaiah 45:12

---
[28] Isaiah 45:12.

> For instance, Paul mentions elect angels in 1 Timothy 5:21 and says that one star is different from another star in glory (remember that they believed the stars, the sun, and the moon were heavenly creatures there to glorify God):

The Scripture in 1 Corinthians implies that each star (which is frequently the identification of angels within the Bible,[29] is unique in glory and position of authority, which the late Billy Graham firmly believed as well.

> *"There is one glory of the sun, and another glory of the moon, and another glory of the stars; for star differs from star in glory."* 1 Corinthians 15:41

Therefore, although speculative, theologians centuries ago divided the angelic beings into nine types of angels within three major groups known as choirs (see image).[f] This is also taught within the Catholic Church, where they believe in the choirs and the angels having different spheres of influence. So, while we may be able to speak directly to God through prayer and our relationship with Christ, according to the Bible, God reaches us through His various angels, each with distinct duties in God's beautiful plan.

I wish we could **all** see the different types of angels and what they specifically look like. Although Scripture describes some of them, sadly, when I looked at pictures online, nothing did them justice compared to what I have seen with some angels. I guess there are many things created by God that are indescribable within our remit of language. However, as we read the Scriptures, you'll hopefully get a clearer picture of some of them.

---

[29] Job 38:7 and Revelation 12:4.

Chapter 3 - Understanding Divine Assignments   49

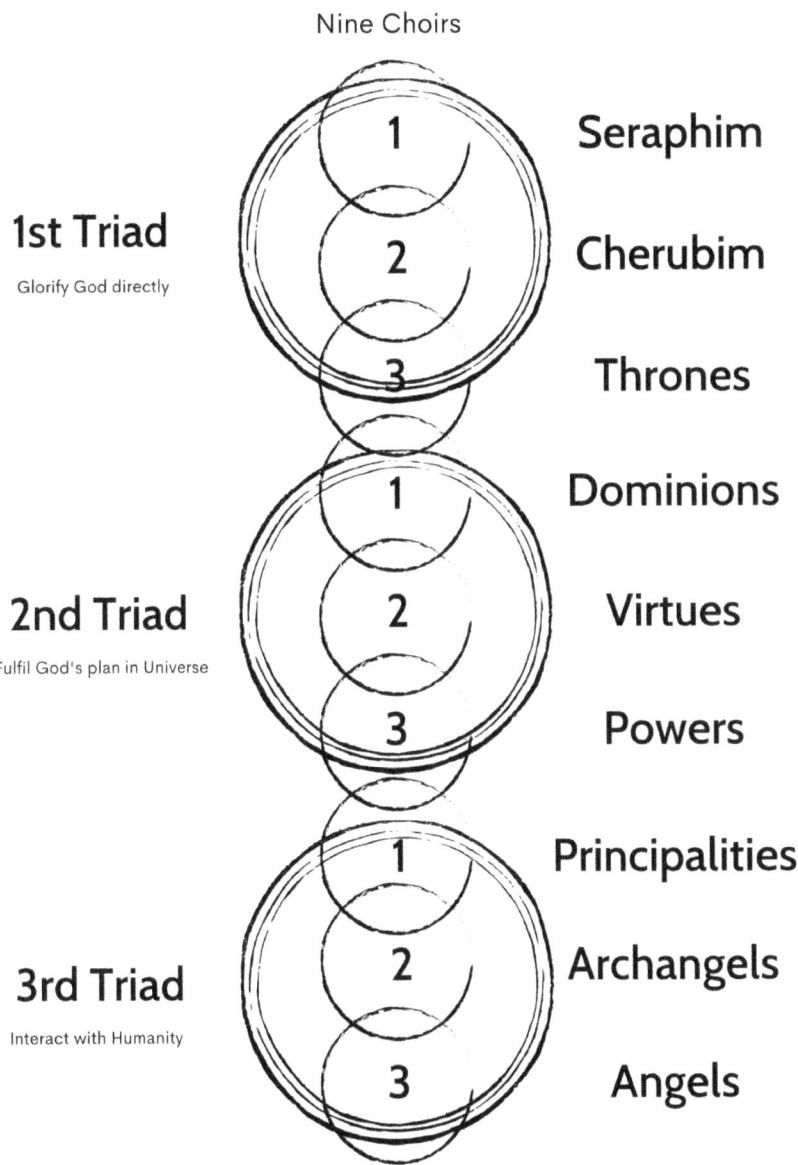

If I were a betting person, I'd say that if I asked you to picture an angel right now, most would imagine naked cherubs—chubby, winged babies like those depicted in Renaissance paintings from the 15th and 16th centuries in Europe. Or perhaps you'd think of men with wings, or people with halos, because that's how we've been conditioned to visualise angels. Yet, none of these images are found in the Bible.

Indeed, the Bible often presents angels as appearing in human form. However, this does not indicate that angels, in their essence, resemble us, because they are spiritual beings with no physical body. This means, as spiritual beings, it is unclear why the angels would require wings (that we like to think of them as having). Angels are not bound by the laws of the physical universe, so they do not need wings to fly. Although we commonly picture them with wings, most angels described in Scripture are not depicted this way. It's worth remembering that. Yes, some do, and I'll go into this. However, we need to be open to the fact that we will not understand everything angels can or cannot do because we have limited understanding and knowledge.

Ultimately, going back to the different choirs—whether you believe that choirs exist or not—what we can be sure of is that angels were created to serve God's purposes. Although Scripture gives us glimpses into the supernatural realm, it should be enough to learn that angels perform various tasks and are used differently by God and Him alone.

So, in the first choir, they are said to contemplate and adore God directly. In other words, these angels are the nearest angels to God's presence.

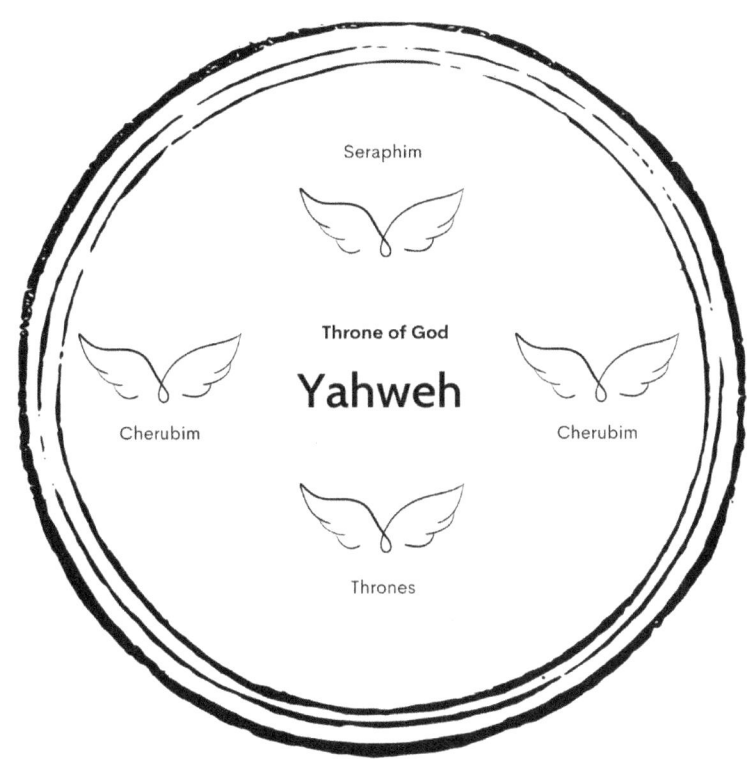

1. Seraphim (Seraph in singular form)

Seraphim is simply a word that means "fiery", "bright", or "burning ones." Seraphim attend to the Throne of God, and Seraphim are the angels mentioned as angelic beings within the Book of Isaiah 6:1-4:

> *"Above him were seraphim, each with six wings: With two wings they covered their faces, with two they covered their feet, and with two they were flying. And they were calling to one another: 'Holy, holy, holy is the Lord Almighty; the whole earth is full of his glory.' At the sound of their voices the doorposts and thresholds shook and the temple was filled with smoke."*

Scripture shows us they have six wings: two to fly with or move around, and two to cover their face because they are in the presence of the Lord (which is a great reminder that even the angels cannot look directly at Yahweh). They also have two wings to cover their feet, which evokes an image of a culture where showing one's feet, especially the sole of their feet, to another person is considered a mark of disrespect. Yet, this makes more sense when we understand that Seraphs are positioned directly above the Throne of God. They are angels focused on obeying God and continually worshipping His name and character, which is awesome! As a side note, these are the types of angels who purified Isaiah by touching coal from God's throne on Isaiah's lips as he began his prophetic ministry. However, it is important to note that the seraphim only interact with him because Isaiah has been taken up into that heavenly realm. In other words, the seraph does not come down—Isaiah is lifted up into the third heaven. That's how it works. Seraphim aren't sent to Earth. They stay where God is, because they want nothing more than to be permanently in the weight of His glory.

Isaiah Chapter 6 is the only place in the Bible that explicitly mentions seraphim. The seraphim fly about the throne on which God is seated, singing His praises as they call special attention to God's glory and majesty.

Scripture also shows that they have the three-fold repetition of calling "Holy, holy, holy is the Lord Almighty," called in Greek a *trihagion*. They call or cry out to one another because they are expressing, with force and passion, the truth of God's supreme holiness. A trihagion also expresses God's triune nature—that is, the three persons of the Godhead… The Father, the Son, and the Holy Spirit, are all equal in holiness and majesty.

Have you ever taken notice of how God is so detailed? Nothing is by chance, and so, in the Old Testament, where Isaiah had a vision, and when John has his vision in the New Testament in the book of

Revelation, the Seraphim (in both visions) are crying out, "Holy, Holy, Holy" which indicates that our God is the same in both testaments. So many people think of God in the Old Testament as a God of Wrath, and the God of the New Testament as the God of love and grace. Still, Isaiah and John present a unified picture that our Holy, Majestic, and Awesome God does not change,[30] and therefore, He is the same yesterday, today and forever.[31]

2. Cherubim (Cherub in singular form)

Their name means the "fullness of wisdom", but these angels stand beside God's throne, unlike the Seraphim, who are above. Therefore, they share one thing in common with the Seraphim; constantly glorifying God by being involved in His worship and praise.

The Cherubim are mentioned numerous times within Scripture, with the first time being after Adam and Eve were driven out of the Garden of Eden; the cherubim were placed there to guard the entrance, not to punish humanity but to guard what was still holy. Eden was the place where heaven touched earth and God walked with His creation. Even after the fall, His presence remained. And the cherubim were set at the edge—meaning this was not done for us, but for the Father, because Cherubim are guardians of holy places.

> *"After He drove the man out, He placed on the east side of the Garden of Eden cherubim and a flaming sword flashing back and forth to guard the way to the tree of life."* Genesis 3:24

Yet, in most of the Scripture, cherubim are mentioned in connection with the Ark of the Covenant. Two cherubim adorned the cover[32] of the ark to protect and guard the holiness and power of God, but their presence always represents God's abiding presence with His people, but also, God's presence is holy ground. So, every time cherubim show up after that, it's the same story. They're overshadowing the mercy seat in the tabernacle. They're surrounding Him in the

---

[30] Malachi 3:6.   [31] Hebrews 13:8.   [32] Exodus 25:18-21.

Book of Revelation. Always with Him. Always glorifying. Never wandering. They weren't created to interact with us. They were created to be near Him. And I believe that tells us something. His glory isn't casual. God's presence isn't something to treat lightly. Even the holiest beings cover their faces before Him. They remind us that God isn't just "close" or "friendly." He's holy. He's weighty. He's unlike anything else. And He deserves the kind of worship that doesn't get tired—worship that never moves on to something else.

Also, when Ezekiel sees the glory of God leaving the temple, he also sees cherubim carrying the throne of God,[33] and the description was:

> *"And every one had four faces: the first face was the face of the cherub, and the second face was a human face, and the third the face of a lion, and the fourth the face of an eagle."* Ezekiel 10:14

In his book, Ezekiel also describes them as completely covered with eyes, from the top of their heads to the tips of their glowing calf-like feet. Their human-shaped hands are also tucked inside each of their four wings[34] —so they are most definitely not the chubby babies people think cherubim are!!!

Let's read to be sure:

> Ezekiel 1:8 says, *"Under their wings on their four sides they had human hands. And the four had their faces and their wings thus."*

> Ezekiel 10:7-8 says, *"And a cherub stretched out his hand from between the cherubim to the fire that was between the cherubim, and took some of it and put it into the hands of the man clothed in linen, who took it and went out. The cherubim appeared to have the form of a human hand under their wings."*

> Ezekiel 10:21 says, *"Each had four faces, and each four wings, and underneath their wings the likeness of human hands."*

---

[33] Ezekiel 10. [34] Ezekiel 1:8,10:7-8, 21.

3. Thrones (or Ophanim)

Again, these next angels will not represent what we deem angels to look like. Thrones are said to show God's power, glory, and judgement, but they appear, from what Ezekiel states, as flaming, rotating rings covered in eyes.

In Ezekiel Chapter One, he is not only captivated, but I imagine just a tad terrified as well, by the image of the massive cherubim floating towards him in this vision. The cherubim are floating, but they are also speeding back and forth like lightning, or flashes, in the sole direction of God's Spirit. Yet, Ezekiel then notices a wheel beneath each Cherub, and he says this:

> *"This was the appearance and structure of the wheels: They sparkled like topaz, and all four looked alike. Each appeared to be made like a wheel intersecting a wheel. As they moved, they would go in any one of the four directions the creatures faced; the wheels did not change direction as the creatures went. Their rims were high and awesome, and all four rims were full of eyes all around."* Ezekiel 1:16-18

These "creatures" are known as Thrones or Ophanim after the ancient Hebrew word meaning "wheels", but the cherubim and thrones are thought to be one symbiotic entity and spread above the heads of the four cherubim. Ophanim is a crystal vault that is so breathtaking that the only human word Ezekiel has is "awesome"…

> *"Spread out above the heads of the living creatures was what looked something like a vault, sparkling like crystal, and awesome. Under the vault their wings were stretched out one toward the other, and each had two wings covering its body. When the creatures moved, I heard the sound of their wings, like the roar of rushing waters, like the voice of the Almighty, like the tumult of an army. When they stood still, they lowered their wings.*

> *Then there came a voice from above the vault over their heads as they stood with lowered wings. Above the vault over their heads was what looked like a throne of lapis lazuli, and high above on the throne was a figure like that of a man. I saw that from what appeared to be his waist up he looked like glowing metal, as if full of fire, and that from there down he looked like fire; and brilliant light surrounded him. Like the appearance of a rainbow in the clouds on a rainy day, so was the radiance around him.*
>
> *This was the appearance of the likeness of the glory of the Lord. When I saw it, I fell facedown, and I heard the voice of one speaking."* Ezekiel 1:22-28

Note: The Bible does not specifically reference the Ophanim or Thrones as angelic beings. However, Jewish apocalyptic writers do (along with Enoch), whereby they list them as a class of angels, along with the Seraphim and Cherubim within the first choir, simply because of their supernatural power and proximity to God's throne.

Congregations also sing traditional Jewish prayers about the ophanim during their Shabbat morning service. This is from text taken from the Dead Sea Scrolls and the Book of Enoch, which, if you remember from the earlier chapter, is not classed as part of the Canon of Scripture we have, so it's more historical or to be used as a reference. Yet, these texts also describe the Ophanim as angelic beings who never sleep while guarding the throne of God. Therefore, whether the thrones are angels or not, I believe they ultimately had a role in revealing God's glory to Ezekiel. However, the Bible also reaffirms that everything points to Jesus.

> *"For by him were all things created, that are in heaven, and that are in earth, visible and invisible, whether they be thrones, or dominions, or principalities, or powers: all things were created by him, and for him."* Colossians 1:16 KJV

Thrones serve as God's chariot and dispense his judgement to fulfil His desires for us. Some people believe thrones are angels of pure submission and humility because God sits upon them.

Yet, since thrones are the lowest of the first angelic choir, they exist at a point where heaven intersects creation. Thus, thrones are believed to offer the lower angels access to God's wisdom. Thrones are also considered heavenly governors because the second choir balances good and bad in fulfilling God's plan for the Universe.

So, here's what we can take from that: whether Thrones are wheels of fire or even heavenly governors, their role is to bear up the glory of God's throne and to display His justice, His power, and His rule. And that's exactly what Thrones remind us of: God's glory is awesome, overwhelming, and it always points us back to Him.

Lastly, one thing to notice in the Scripture we just read in Colossians is that this letter from Paul[35] refers to angelic powers; one from the first triad (thrones), one from the third triad (principalities), and two choirs out of the second triad (dominions and powers).

So, let's look at the second triad now.

Note: These next angels don't have much information written about them.

4. Dominions

These are the angels who are govern over the lower angels and humanity. Ultimately, they govern the Universe, so they control the stars and planets under God's authority. The name "dominion" comes from the Latin "domination" and the Greek "kyriotetes" for "lordship," which shows their role in supervising angels below them. This shows us that these angels have a role of oversight and supervision. They exercise dominion, not as a replacement of God's authority, but as those governing under His command.

---

[35] Colossians 1:16.

So, while Cherubim guard holiness and Thrones bear God's glory, the Dominions ensure the ongoing order of creation and the balance of God's plan.

In Scripture, we can see them named again in the Book of Ephesians:

> *"Far above all rule and authority and power and dominion, and above every name that is named, not only in this age but also in the one to come."* Ephesians 1:21

I want to break down this incredible verse because sometimes we can gloss over these things. This is what I believe Paul is saying:

Far above all rule and authority (in this world) and power and dominion (in the universe – which, remember, powers and dominions are two of the angels in the second triad), no matter if it is people ruling or angels overseeing the universe, Christ is above every name that is named—not only in this age but also in the one to come.

5. Virtues

The next ones are Virtues, and these angels are slightly different because, unlike cherubim or seraphim, they don't appear in a physical form in the way we'd picture angels, so these angels we would often use to refer to actions, not to "living" angelic beings. In other words, when Scripture and tradition talk about Virtues, it's not describing a figure with wings, or fire, but a kind of angelic order that embodies God's strength and His power at work in the world.

This is because the Virtues are said to be the agents of God's miracles. When God steps into creation to do the impossible — to heal, to deliver, to part seas, to raise the dead — the Virtues are involved. They are like channels of divine perfection, carrying the energy of heaven into the brokenness of earth.

Perfection is part of the meaning of the word "virtue," which is "vertus" in Latin, but it also refers to excellence and courage.

We will understand virtues, more commonly known as "strongholds" within our lives, because of their immovable strength. I will speak about the angelic rebellion in the next chapter. Still, Scripture shows us that a third of the angels chose to follow satan into darkness. Some people really focus on this, yet it's remembering that within all of the different types of angels, we have two-thirds still doing the will of God.

So, virtues signify certain powerful and unshakable Godlike energies, but we tend to think of strongholds as bad, especially with the term stronghold appearing at least fifty times in the Bible, and within that, it is commonly referred to as a fortress with difficult access. The Apostle Paul uses the term to describe a mindset or attitude.

> *"For though we live in the world, we do not wage war as the world does. The weapons we fight with are not the weapons of the world. On the contrary, they have divine power to demolish strongholds. We demolish arguments and every pretension that sets itself up against the knowledge of God, and we take captive every thought to make it obedient to Christ. And we will be ready to punish every act of disobedience, once your obedience is complete."* 2 Corinthians 10:3-6

Yet, virtues are good too, and we, therefore, should begin to think of God's stronghold in the way described in Psalm 9:9:

> *"The Lord is a refuge for the oppressed, a stronghold in times of trouble."*

Do you see the difference? The devil's strongholds bind you; God's stronghold protects you.

So, when we talk about the angels called Virtues, think of them as representing the immovable strength of God's stronghold. They are unshakable, steadfast, unmovable — embodying the refuge of God. Therefore, Virtues remind us of this truth: God's power is greater. His stronghold is sure. And when He moves, He doesn't just demolish the enemy's strongholds — He becomes *our stronghold.*

6. Powers

The strength of the virtues, in turn, leads us to that of the next choir of angels, called "the powers," also known in Scripture as "the authorities" found in Ephesians. Now, these angels are not unlike the authorities we know (such as police officers) because these powers or authorities have the power to control evil spirits that torment those on earth, and to thwart their plans.

The name "powers" comes from the Latin "potestas" (meaning authority), which, in turn, comes from the Greek "exousia", which refers to "someone whose will must be obeyed." These are not weak angels. These are angels of command.

These angels are certainly not to be ignored, and they are said to assist in governing the natural order. So, these are the ones who go to war against the demonic choirs (again, more on this in the next chapter), but powers are said to direct the lower angels in battles against the forces of hell. Powers also oversee the power that human beings have— such as kings, government officials, etc.—that have been given in the world.

These angels are the ones generally shown wearing armour and carrying swords, armed for battle—hence why we can read about them in the well-known Spiritual Warfare passage of Ephesians 6:12;

> *"For our struggle is not against flesh and blood, but against the rulers, against the authorities, against the powers of this dark world and against the spiritual forces of evil in the heavenly realms."*

Remember, Paul here is saying that the real fight isn't with people. It's not flesh and blood. It's with spiritual powers. Some of those have fallen, aligned with satan. But there are also faithful Powers — God's warrior angels — who stand against them and enforce His rule in the spiritual realm. In other words, these warrior angels don't just fight battles in the unseen; they coordinate with the angels who bring God's word and direction to people like you and me.

So, think of Daniel chapter 10, where he was fasting for 21 days in the wilderness, and he received no word from God and Scripture tells us that the angels were battling – those were powers, and Michael came to help them in the end in order to get the message to him. But this passage is incredible, and it should remind us of two things. First: our fight is real. The unseen war is raging all around us. But second, we are not left defenceless. God has assigned Powers to restrain evil, to fight back darkness, and to keep order even in the middle of chaos. So, when you feel pressed, when you feel attacked, remember: you are not wrestling alone. Heaven's army is active. The Powers are on assignment, and the authority of Jesus Christ is above them all.

Lastly, since powers are on the "lowest rank" of this second triad of angels, they interact most closely with the last three choirs of angels—the messengers, and so, this leads us to the third and final triad of choirs, in which these angels interact and serve humanity closely through God's will and direction. However, just like the previous choirs, angels in this triad interact most closely with those in the ranks above them. In other words, the lowest rank of the angels of government—the powers—are believed to interact most closely with the upper rank of the messenger angels, the principalities.

7. Principalities

If Powers oversee battles and restrain evil, then Principalities are those who watch over groups of people, leaders, and even nations. Their role is to protect earthly structures, guide communities, and influence leaders toward good works. You might think of them like army generals or office managers—directing those under their care. In this way, Principalities guide the archangels and messenger angels, ensuring God's purposes reach the right people at the right time. Some also suggest that the Principalities may be included among the 'angels of the seven churches' mentioned in Revelation 2–3.

The phrase principalities and powers occurs six times together in the Bible and always within the King James Version. Other versions translate it variously as "rulers and authorities," "forces and authorities," and "rulers and powers." So, when I study the angelic realm in Scripture, I primarily read from the King James Version, along with the English Standard Version and the New International Version. I also consult the Interlinear Bible, since it provides a direct word-for-word rendering of the original Hebrew and Greek texts.

King James Version

In most places where these phrases appear, the contexts make it clear that they refer to the vast array of evil and malicious spirits who make war against the people of God. An example of this would be in Ephesians 6:12, and yes, that's the bad side of the picture. Fallen principalities are part of the chaos, stirring up rebellion, influencing leaders, and working against everything God is doing. But again, and this is important to remember that for every fallen principality, there are twice as many loyal ones still serving God. And those faithful Principalities are still at work, guiding nations, strengthening leaders, and protecting the people of God.

Now, for those of you who think that principalities are just evil and demonic, and you cannot see that what I am saying is true, let's head over to the final reference to principalities and powers from the Book of Titus:

"Put them in mind to be subject to principalities and powers, to obey magistrates, to be ready to every good work." Titus 3:1 KJV *"Teach your people to obey the leaders of their country. They should be ready to do any good work."* Titus 3:1 NLT

Do you see the two layers here? On one hand, it's about earthly rulers and authorities. But in the King James Version, Paul also points to the spiritual layer — the angelic principalities and powers that God has appointed as His representatives in the unseen realm.

So, here, people can read this verse and assume it refers to those governmental authorities God has placed over us for our protection and welfare. Often, humanity refuses to submit to those in control. Yet, the King James Version shows what is happening in the Spiritual Realm – because humanity is subject to the angelic realm, which are God's representatives on earth. Again, we will revisit this a couple of chapters from now because, contrary to what some believe, angels are not subject to us at this time, but are submissive only to God. So, those who rebel against earthly authorities are actually rebelling against what God has instituted, and those who do so, Scripture tells us, "Will bring judgement on themselves."[36]

So, here's the point: when we resist godly authority on earth, we're actually resisting the spiritual order God has put in place. Romans Chapter 13 makes the same point: those who rebel against authority "bring judgment on themselves."

Thus, Principalities remind us that heaven is structured. God is a God of order. There are angels overseeing nations, cities, and churches — and when those leaders yield to God, His blessing flows. When they resist Him, there's turmoil. So, the takeaway is this: don't just pray for yourself — pray for your leaders. Pray for your nation. Pray for your church, because Principalities are working in the unseen realm, but God's people on earth must align with that order through obedience and prayer.

---

[36] Romans 13:2.

8. Archangels

The next choir is the angels, whom we briefly mentioned in the last chapter. Below the principalities come the archangels, or as they are also known, the princes of angels. We probably know of these angels best of all, but the word *archangel* occurs in only two verses of the Bible:

> *"For the Lord himself will come down from heaven, with a loud command, with the voice of the archangel and with the trumpet call of God, and the dead in Christ will rise first."* 1 Thessalonians 4:16

And,

> *"But even the archangel Michael, when he was disputing with the devil about the body of Moses, did not himself dare to condemn him for slander but said, "The Lord rebuke you!"* Jude 1:9

Archangel comes from a Greek word, "*archangelos*", meaning "chief angel." These types of angels are assigned to communicate and carry out God's important plans for humanity. As mentioned previously, angels possess intelligence, power, and glory, but as always, archangels serve God and carry out His purposes.

We also know that there is more than one Archangel from the Dead Sea Scrolls and other historical books, although our canon of Scripture only tells us of one—Michael—but Scripture implies there is more because of the verse found in Daniel:

> *"But the prince of the Persian kingdom resisted me twenty-one days. Then Michael, one of the chief princes, came to help me, because I was detained there with the king of Persia."* Daniel 10:13

This places Michael on the same level as the other "chief princes," but even if there are multiple archangels, it is believed that Michael is the chief among them because he is the only one named.

We also know from sources such as the Book of Tobit (again, I reiterate, this is not from the canon of Scripture, so this is just informative) that there are apparently seven in all who serve as divine ambassadors and warrior chiefs. So, we would have seen in artwork that the archangels wear armour with shields and have a sword and generally look like men. Still, ultimately, the artwork is correct, because archangels are charged with engaging in Spiritual Warfare, amongst other things.

Michael oversees the Jewish people, as noted in Daniel 10:21 and Daniel 12:1, so it is believed that perhaps other archangels are given the task of protecting other nations. Still, Scripture does not identify this, and that is the important thing to remember. If God wanted us to know who the archangels are (meaning the plural), He would have made sure that it was noted within the Bible we have.

> Daniel 10:21 *"First I will tell you what is written in the Book of Truth. No one supports me against them except Michael, your prince."*
>
> Daniel 12:1 *"At that time Michael, the great prince who protects your people, will arise. There will be a time of distress such as has not happened from the beginning of nations until then. But at that time your people—everyone whose name is found written in the book—will be delivered."*

In 1 Thessalonians 4:16,[37] an archangel is involved in the return of Christ to His Church. We also see Michael (archangel) contending with satan in the Book of Jude. Even though he possesses the power and glory of an archangel, Michael called on the Lord to rebuke satan. This just shows how much we shouldn't underestimate satan, but it is a good reminder as well, as to how dependent Michael is on God's power, so we should be too.

---

[37] 1 Thessalonians 4:16.

We also know fallen angels seem to have "territories" as well because Daniel mentions a spiritual "prince of Greece" and a spiritual "prince of Persia" who opposed the holy angel who brought the message to Daniel when he fasted for 21 days.[38]

Lastly, Michael is often shown in pictures as the one slaying a dragon, which is a reminder of his role in the battle that drove the fallen angels from heaven:

> *"Then war broke out in heaven. Michael and his angels fought against the dragon, and the dragon and his angels fought back. But he was not strong enough, and they lost their place in heaven. The great dragon was hurled down—that ancient serpent called the devil, or Satan, who leads the whole world astray. He was hurled to the earth, and his angels with him."* Revelation 12:7

And whilst archangels are listed as eighth in the nine choirs of angels, Michael is considered the battle commander of all the angels. This is because of his zeal against satan in the war in heaven.

Now, there are two lessons here, I believe:

1) Michael didn't fight in his own strength. In Jude 1:9, even when confronting the devil, Michael didn't stand in arrogance. He said, "The Lord rebuke you." Even the mightiest warrior in heaven depends completely on the power of God. How much more should we?

2) Michael reminds us that the battle is real, but it's also already won. Satan was cast down. Christ reigns above all. And when Jesus returns, it will be with the voice of the archangel — a declaration that history's war has reached its end, and the King is coming for His people.

---

[38] Daniel 10:20.

So, Archangels point us to this truth: God never leaves His people unprotected. He has assigned warrior princes, battle commanders like Michael, to fight for His people and to carry His most urgent messages. But even they are subject to Christ, the Lord of hosts.

I wanted to add here that within the hierarchy of the angels, it doesn't mean that one angel is weaker than the other; it is purely about the placement of where they stand in relation to God and man, because God is Righteous and Holy, and we are not, until sanctification is complete, when Jesus returns.

9. Angels

This then takes us to the final choir of the angels. They are called the lowest in the ranks, but again, this has more to do with their interactions on Earth, rather than their value or importance. There is no number to these angels. They exist in myriads (which means too many to count), and these types of angels include the heavenly choirs and guardian angels, as mentioned in Matthew 18:10:

> *"See that you do not despise one of these little ones. For I tell you that their angels in heaven always see the face of my Father in heaven."*

We all know how angels have been represented within the world, which are generally with wings to signify their role as messengers, with flowing robes and shining faces that reflect God's glory; but generally, angels are spiritual beings and will only take the form of a man if directed by God because they are His servants.

Psalm Chapter 103:19-21 gives us further information on this:

> *"The Lord has established his throne in heaven, and his kingdom rules over all. Praise the Lord, you his angels, you mighty ones who do his bidding, who obey his word. Praise the Lord, all his heavenly hosts, you his servants who do his will."*

In this passage, the psalmist praises God for the extent of divine authority—think about it, no part of creation is not under God's rule; His throne has been "established."

The heavenly hosts praise the Lord and are, in fact, God's servants who are at His "beck and call." They dutifully obey God's commands, carry out His bidding, and fulfil His will. As believers, we will someday inhabit heaven with God and the heavenly hosts, as the book of Hebrews states:

> *"But you have come to Mount Zion, to the city of the living God, the heavenly Jerusalem. You have come to thousands upon thousands of angels in joyful assembly."* Hebrews 12:22

Imagine that: countless angels, gathered in joy around the throne of God — and yet, some of them are sent specifically to watch over you. That's where I believe we get the idea of guardian angels, because these angels are assigned to protect God's people, especially the vulnerable. Isn't that incredible? At the same time, these types of angels are watching over us, they are also gazing into the face of the Father — meaning they are always ready to carry out His will on our behalf. Remember, angels are not floating around with harps, waiting to be entertained. They are mighty ones who obey God's word. They are servants at God's command, carrying out His purposes in creation and in our lives, and while culture often pictures them with robes, wings, and glowing faces, Scripture shows us something more profound. They are spiritual beings, who sometimes appear in human form only when God directs them. Hebrews 13:2 even warns us that some of us have "entertained angels unaware" — meaning they can walk among us when God sends them on assignment.

But here's another point to consider: When Jesus returns, remember that we will not become angels when we go to Heaven, but will be with them, in glory, for all of eternity, but humanity will not become them. I have had so many conversations around this misconception!

Jesus didn't die to make us angels — He died to make us children of God, sons and daughters, co-heirs with Christ. Yet, the angels will be there with us, worshiping the Lamb, carrying out His commands, and filling heaven with joy.

So Ministering Angels remind us of this: you are never alone. God's heavenly hosts are active, carrying out His will, protecting His people, and ensuring His plan comes to pass, and one day, when Christ returns, those same angels will accompany Him in glory. I will actually discuss this choir of angels more in a later chapter, as they have many roles on earth, ensuring that God's perfect plan comes to fruition for humanity.

So, when you put these nine types of angels together, here's the bigger picture:

- **The Worshippers**
  - declaring His holiness.

- **The Messengers**
  - delivering His Word.

- **The Servants and Protectors**
  - strengthening and guarding His people.

- **The Warriors**
  - contending with darkness under Christ's authority.

- **The Witnesses**
  - watching, recording, glorifying God's plan unfolding.

And here's what we cannot miss: every one of these roles points us back to God.

Their worship reveals His holiness.

Their protection reveals His care.

Their warfare reveals His authority.

Their witness reveals His sovereignty.

Angels know their place. They are servants. Jesus is the Saviour. So, here's what this means for us: The unseen realm is structured. Angels are on assignment. But the whole point is not to get caught up in their ranks and titles. The point is to see that our God rules the unseen realm. And if He rules the unseen realm, then He also rules the seen, and if He commands His angels, then surely, we are all good, no matter what life throws at us.

CHAPTER FOUR

Rebellion of satan

"You alone are the LORD. You made the heavens, even the highest heavens, and all their starry host, the earth and all that's on it."
Nehemiah 9:6

Scripture doesn't specifically tell us when angels were created, yet we know from Scripture that angels were created by God and for Him.[39] We can also read from Scripture that angels existed before the earth's foundation was laid because, in the book of Job, God asks him where he was when God laid the foundation and when the morning stars sang together, and all the angels shouted for joy.[40]

Therefore, one thing that we can beconfident about is that God created the angels before humans were formed on day six of creation, because God reflected at the end of that day and said:

> *"Thus the heavens and the earth were finished, and all the host of them."* Genesis 2:1 KJV

Now, I briefly touched on this within the last chapter, but one-third of all angels created fell when satan was cast out of Heaven by Michael (Archangel). Therefore, I want to go into lucifer and his demonic angels, along with the rebellion, within this chapter. I do believe that humanity has grasped this incorrectly, misunderstanding the amount of power that satan has over us and the things that the demonic can do to us.

---

[39] Colossians 1:16-17.   [40] Job 38:4,7.

Now, I thought the easiest way to go into all things "demonic" was to start from the beginning, when satan—or lucifer as he was known then—was still in heaven.

But firstly, we need to think about the reality that the world struggles with the subject of angels, and they also seem to struggle to understand the demonic (or demons). The term "demons" is mentioned over eighty times in the New Testament, so Christians cannot ignore this topic. Yet, it is also not healthy to dwell on them too much because of our authority in Christ, which we will discuss in the next chapter.

So, we should now understand that angels are God's messengers who were created early within the seven days of creation, most likely on day two. The book of Genesis reveals that God's opinion of His work was "very good" when looking over all that He had done. Therefore, because of God's nature or because His very essence is goodness, we need to conclude that God did not create demons or evil in this world.

Again, Scripture does not elaborate on when the demonic or evil first appeared on the earth, but we know that they came after the world was created and God declared His work was good in Genesis chapter one. Therefore, it was somewhere between then and before satan tempted Eve in chapter three, when they were still within the Garden of Eden.

We must go to the Book of Isaiah to understand lucifer's downfall, because he was created perfectly. Scripture tells us that he was the most beautiful thing created in heaven, which we will look at shortly. Some believe that he was probably the ruling prince of the Universe under God.

Yet, angels have freewill as well; in other words, they all have the choice to sin, or not, just like us. And because of lucifer's desire to be like God, it was no longer good enough for him to be a perfectly created angel in the beauty and presence of God, so let me turn your attention to Isaiah 14:

> *"How you have fallen from heaven, morning star, son of the dawn! You have been cast down to the earth, you who once laid low the nations! You said in your heart, "I will ascend to the heavens, I will raise my throne above the stars of God; I will sit enthroned on the mount of assembly, on the utmost heights of Mount Zaphon. I will ascend above the tops of the clouds; I will make myself like the Most High." But you are brought down to the realm of the dead, to the depths of the pit."* Isaiah 14:12-15

So, lucifer's rebellion resulted in a war in Heaven, which has been going on since he was thrown out to earth. Do you see where his heart was…

I will ascend to the Heavens.

I will raise my throne above the stars of God. Remember that stars represent the names given to angels in Scripture, so he was saying that his angels would be above God's.

I will sit enthroned on the mount of assembly—in other words, he will sit higher than God.

I will ascend above the tops of the clouds.

And this last one…*I will* make myself like the Most High.

Lucifer declared what was within his heart five times, which was to be greater than God. He wanted to be the centre of power throughout the Universe.

Let's face it; an *"I will"* spirit ultimately has a spirit of rebellion because where is God in all this? Lucifer wanted to be worshipped, just like this world has seen in many others. Hence, why satan is the prince of this world; humanity doesn't want to worship God—they want to be worshipped. We want power and glory.

The power of "I"—I want, I need, I should have—is dangerous, because this covetousness is evil, and the desire to want what others have is the root of wars, anger, destruction, frustration, and greed.

As mentioned, angels, being created by God, have the same attributes as us, so they have the freedom to choose. Instead of being humble and obedient, satan chose *pride*.

> Proverbs 16:18 *says, "Pride goes before destruction and a haughty spirit before a fall."*

In other words, pride and arrogance will destroy you. Like lucifer, the most beautiful, powerful angel, who wanted more. So, let's look at who lucifer was from the book of Ezekiel:

> *"You were the seal of perfection, full of wisdom and perfect in beauty. You were in Eden, the garden of God; every precious stone adorned you: carnelian, chrysolite and emerald, topaz, onyx and jasper, lapis lazuli, turquoise and beryl. Your settings and mountings were made of gold; on the day you were created they were prepared. You were anointed as a guardian cherub, for so I ordained you. You were on the holy mount of God; you walked among the fiery stones. You were blameless in your ways from the day you were created till wickedness was found in you. Through your widespread trade you were filled with violence, and you sinned. So I drove you in disgrace from the mount of God, and I expelled you, guardian cherub, from among the fiery stones. Your heart became proud on account of your beauty, and you corrupted your wisdom because of your splendour. So I threw you to the earth; I made a spectacle of you before kings."*
> Ezekiel 28:12-17

Ok, so let's remember the last chapter and the picture that helps us visualise God's Throne and the position of the angels. This Scripture, found in Ezekiel, shows us that lucifer was a cherub. This means that he walked amongst the fiery stones on the holy mount of God.

In other words, lucifer was next to God. Lucifer was beside Yahweh, because he was blameless, perfect because of his splendour, and he was a wise angel. But that was still not enough! Satan wanted to be on that throne and to be worshipped, so God threw him and a third of his angels who followed satan to earth to make a spectacle of him.

This is why his anger has raged since then. He hates anything to do with God, which is why he hates Christians so much. So, from this point, lucifer became satan…the devil…the deceiver…the one who wants to destroy all who love God.

We can read when satan got thrown out of the third heaven by going over to the Book of Revelation:

> *"Then another sign appeared in heaven: an enormous red dragon with seven heads and ten horns and seven crowns on its heads. Its tail swept a third of the stars out of the sky and flung them to the earth. The dragon stood in front of the woman who was about to give birth, so that it might devour her child the moment he was born. Then war broke out in heaven. Michael and his angels fought against the dragon, and the dragon and his angels fought back. But he was not strong enough, and they lost their place in heaven. The great dragon was hurled down—that ancient serpent called the devil, or Satan, who leads the whole world astray. He was hurled to the earth, and his angels with him."* Revelation 12:3-4,7-9

Imagine a third of the stars of heaven being thrown to the earth along with satan. Within Scripture, you will often see that we can have partial fulfilment and complete fulfilment of prophecy regarding things that occur within Scripture. But with this passage, the partial fulfilment is when satan was cast out of the third heaven, and the complete fulfilment will be when Jesus returns, and satan and his minions are thrown into the lake of fire once and for all as their final judgement.

In case you were wondering, in 2 Corinthians 12:2-3, Apostle Paul provides a major revelation that there are three "heavens." This passage discusses being taken to the third heaven, where God the Father and Jesus reside.

First Heaven

The first heaven is our atmosphere or air, which is found in Genesis 6:7. The word translated from "air" is "ouranos," the same Greek word that is elsewhere translated as "heaven," found in Matthew 6:26.

Second Heaven

The second heaven is the universe or outer space as we know it, which includes the sun, moon, and stars, and therefore, is known as the Celestial Heaven referred to in Matthew 24:29; and Deuteronomy 4:19. Now, we know that the Bible is clear in that God cannot be limited to any one geographical place.[41]

Third Heaven

Scripture also teaches us that there is a specific geographical place where God resides, although it is not revealed where this is; this is the third designated heaven. The writer of Hebrews says:[g]

> *The point of what we are saying is this: We do have such a high priest, who sat down at the right hand of the throne of the Majesty in heaven."* Hebrews 8:1

So, why do I bring the three heavens up?

The Bible indicates that satan and some of his demons are now allowed to move in this space or between the first and second heaven. This means that we can be confident that the first triad of angels are still holy because they are the ones that worship God directly, but in the book of Ephesians 2:1-2, it says:

---

[41] 1 Kings 8:27.

> *"As for you, you were dead in your transgressions and sins, in which you used to live when you followed the ways of this world and of the ruler of the kingdom of the air, the spirit who is now at work in those who are disobedient."*

Therefore, we know that within the second and third triad, in this age, satan and his highest-ranking angels can still oppose the work of God and hinder God's angels. We also know that this occurs because when Daniel was waiting for his prayer to be answered in Daniel 10, he fasted for 21 days. Still, there was Spiritual Warfare during this time, and Michael (archangel) had to intervene in the fighting so that the other angel could bring the news to Daniel.

Relating to the Scripture in Revelation, the complete fulfilment of this battle (which I am not going to get into within this book, as it has to do with End Times), is when satan and the demonic will be removed from the second heaven as well. This is what we call the "Great Tribulation," and this is where satan will be forever banned from his mission of accusation and slander against God's people. His power and freedom will be seriously reduced from this point.

However, I do not believe Christians will experience this part of the world's story, as we will rise to be with Jesus before this happens. Yes, that means that I believe in pre-tribulation, but again, this is end-time stuff, so I will not get into this further (in this book anyway). Yet, whatever happens, whether you are pre-mid-post or tribulation, we know that those inhabitants left on the earth at that time will suffer terribly because satan will be enraged. He will also be aware that he only has three and a half more years until he is bound and cast into hell, so at this point, the earth will usher into a period of intensified suffering, hence the Great Tribulation.[42]

---

[42] Daniel 9:27.

From this, I want to focus on the demonic and what they do. Now, this isn't rocket science, because as I mentioned earlier, demons are the angels who fell with satan. Therefore, these angels are committed to stopping God's will over our lives. These fallen angels also know God is the creator of all, but do not accept Him as an authority over them—this is the difference. Their role, although they have their boundaries (think of the different choirs), is that the demonic do not keep within their domain, and therefore, like Daniel experienced, they obstruct messages from God to try and oppose God's plans.

One of the most damaging ways fallen angels have tried to thwart God's purposes on earth is through the Nephilim. Remember that angels are not male or female in how humans understand and experience gender. But whenever angels are mentioned in the Bible, the word translated as "angel" is always used in the masculine form. Also, when angels appeared to people in the Bible, they were always seen as men. And when they were given names, the names were always masculine.

Scripture indicates that a few fallen angels decided to go way out of their domain and interact with humans in ways God NEVER intended. We will need to read Genesis 6 to see what happened:

> *"When human beings began to increase in number on the earth and daughters were born to them, the sons of God saw that the daughters of humans were beautiful, and they married any of them they chose. The Nephilim were on the earth in those days—and afterwards—when the sons of God went to the daughters of humans and had children by them. They were the heroes of old, men of renown."* Genesis 6:1-2,4

At first glance, what has happened might not be obvious, but the sons of God are angels, which were names given to them in Job 38:4-7 when God was describing His power over creation. And so, these sons of God, i.e., Angels, or the fallen ones, had sex with the daughters of men, i.e., women, due to being filled with lust. This resulted in half-angelic and half-human offspring. These were called "Nephilim" within Scripture.

So, what happened to them?

Well, the Nephilim were one of the primary reasons for the flood in Noah's time. Some people might seem shocked by this revelation. However, historical books such as the Book of Enoch and even the Book of Jubilees (this transcript is also a part of the Dead Sea Scrolls) give information about God ridding the Earth of the Nephilim by flooding it. Now, I know that I have said before about being careful about reading non-canonical books. Still, Jude 14-15 cites from 1 Enoch 1:9. So, commentators believe that although the source Jude uses is not the inspired Word of God, it does contain "truth" that he is willing to use, and therefore, to some commentators, this confirms that Jude regarded the Enochic interpretations as correct. Honestly, we will find out one day, but what we can know for sure is that immediately after the mention of Nephilim, Scripture tells us:

> *"The LORD saw how great man's wickedness on the earth had become, and that every inclination of the thoughts of his heart was only evil all the time. The LORD was grieved that he had made man on the earth, and his heart was filled with pain. So the LORD said, 'I will wipe mankind, whom I have created, from the face of the earth—men and animals, and creatures that move along the ground, and birds of the air— for I am grieved that I have made them."* Genesis 6:5-7

From this, God was grieved so much regarding the violation of His created design that He proceeded to flood the entire earth, killing everyone and everything (including the Nephilim) other than Noah, his family (eight people in total), and the animals on the ark.

Unfortunately, however, demons repeated this sin sometime after the flood. But it likely took place to a much lesser extent than it did before the flood, because if you remember when the Israelites spied out the land of Canaan, they reported back to Moses:

> *"We saw the Nephilim there (the descendants of Anak come from the Nephilim). We seemed like grasshoppers in our own eyes, and we looked the same to them."* Numbers 13:33

So, what prevents the demons from producing more Nephilim today?

It seems that God put an end to demons "mating" with humans by placing all the demons who committed such an act into isolation.

> *"The angels who did not keep their positions of authority but abandoned their own home—these he has kept in darkness, bound with everlasting chains for judgment on the great Day."* Jude 6

In other words, the offending angels were cast down and delivered into chains for judgement.[43] Unfortunately, not all demons are in "prison" today. However, the group of demons who committed this abomination in God's eyes beyond the original "fall" are the ones who are *"bound with everlasting chains."* This is because it prevents any more demons from attempting such things, and the LORD has permanently removed them from our domain.

The last thing I want to look at is the demons who are still free to roam around the world, causing havoc in their paths, but there are three key objectives that satan has with his plan to try and destroy people's love for God. These are demons that deceive, tempt, and destroy.

---

[43] 2 Peter 2:4.

1. Demons deceive

We all know that this has been satan's main plan since the Garden of Eden, as when we hear him speaking, *"you will surely not die,"* it is to deceive. Therefore, deception began to challenge God's goodness and purposes for humanity.

Satan always wanted to make disobedience seem desirable since man was first created, and ultimately, fallen angels wish for as many of us to be thrown into hell as possible because this goes against God's plan that *"none should perish."*

We need to start thinking about demons a tad more, in the sense that they can masquerade as God's faithful angels. Therefore, God has given us discernment for a reason to distinguish between God's truth and satan's lies. Unfortunately, history shows that humanity continues not to do this, giving rise to false religions.

For instance, in 610 AD, Islam was born after Muhammad received the contents of the Koran from visions from someone he thought was the angel, Gabriel. Also, twelve centuries later, Mormonism was created after an apparent angel called Moroni connected Joseph Smith with the Book of Mormon.

Humanity was created to worship, and satan and his minions understand this. Therefore, they are "clever" in many ways because they don't prevent us from worshipping. Instead, they redirect our worship to something other than God.

2. Demons tempt

Think about the Garden of Eden again; satan's deception was coupled with temptation…his words were:

> ***"You will not certainly die***," *(deception) the serpent said to the woman. "For God knows that when you eat from it your eyes will be opened, and **you will be like God** (temptation) knowing good and evil."* Genesis 3:4-5 – emphasis added.

The serpent enticed Eve that when she ate the fruit, she would be like God. Go back to satan's plot when he was in heaven – "I will" …Me…Myself…and I. There is no doubt that satan's sin was rooted in pride from the desire to be like the Most High, and he knew the power that would hold and continues to hold over humanity.

Ultimately, when we worship something other than God, it's idolatry. This is why temptation is closely associated with idolatry and immorality, and in the New Testament, these are the ONLY two sins from which we are told to flee:

> *"Flee sexual immorality."* 1 Corinthians 6:18 *"Flee from idolatry."* 1 Corinthians 10:14

3. Demons destroy

The first two points lead to the reason the demons try to deceive and tempt us—it's all about destroying us. The end game is to stop us from being in heaven and having a relationship with God. This brings to light the Scripture:

> *"The thief comes only to steal and kill and destroy."* John 10:10

Have you ever thought about this? If satan just kills us, then as Jesus' followers, we go to be with the Lord, yet to destroy us means that we end up in hell and outside of God's presence forever.

One of the ways satan destroys humanity is by possessing people. In the New Testament, there are so many accounts of this. There are also so many accounts of humans having incredible power or strength, from a demon possessing them. Amongst other things, there is deafness, convulsions, foaming at the mouth, falling into fire and water, or fierceness—there is no denying that it can be frightening what the demonic can do to humans.

However, I want to point out, and I cannot stress enough, that there are Christians or false teachers who contradict the Word of God because the Bible makes this very clear… I do not believe that a demon can possess any Christian, and here's why… If you are a true believer or a Jesus follower, the Spirit of God dwells within you.

> 1 Corinthians 6:19 says, *"Do you not know that your body is the temple of the Holy Spirit who is in you."*

So, the moment that we become Jesus followers, the Holy Spirit resides in us, and

1 John shows why anyone who says otherwise is incorrect:

> *"You are of God, little children, and have overcome them, because He who is in you is greater than he who is in the world."* 1 John 4:4

The Holy Spirit is more powerful than the demonic and satan (period), and there is not one Scripture that shows us that a Jesus follower is described as demon-possessed in the New Testament.

I believe, and I mean this respectfully, that if someone is demon-possessed, then they may profess with their mouth that Jesus is their saviour. Still, there are some "Christians" who will hear the words *"I never knew you"*[44] when Jesus returns, as they do not actually follow Jesus.

---

[44] Matthew 7:21-23.

Also, we need to understand that there is a clear distinction between demon possession and demon influence. The demonic can "bother us"—this is why James tells us to resist the devil, and he will flee.[45] However, we have the power of the Holy Spirit to help us resist him and overcome any adversity he tries to throw at us.

We only need to think of the passage in Ephesians 6, to see what amazing tools, or even armour, God has given us to protect us and allow us to see victory in our lives.

When Jesus ascended from the grave, every demon, every scheme, every deception, and temptation that satan would throw at us was defeated. So, if we confess and believe, in our hearts, that Jesus is our Lord and Saviour, God will guide and protect us.

I need to add that satan is not to be ignored (as some Christians believe) because he has power within his domain. However, we need to remember that no matter what authority the demonic have right now, it is only granted by God's Sovereignty, and ultimately, it is only for a time because God has the victory—he won the battle when Jesus defeated death.

When I became a Christian, I thought life would be "sweet" once I found God. Yet, we again have this false belief system that life will be cosy. The truth is, we all must cope with being imperfect people in an imperfect world. Accidents, disasters, illness, heartache, loss—the ways the human heart can suffer are countless, and satan knows this and tries to deceive us into believing that God doesn't care. Even Jesus agreed that life wouldn't be simple. He said:

> *"In this world you will have trouble. But take heart! I have overcome the world."* John 16:33

Evil satan and his minions will be cast into hell forever, so we must ensure that we and others do not follow them.

---

[45] James 4:7.

CHAPTER FIVE
Standing with Angels in Spiritual War

"We face dangers every day of which we are not even aware. Often, God intervenes on our behalf through the use of His angels."

Billy Graham

Most people will never see angels—whether the "good or bad" kind—within their lifetime, but that doesn't change the fact that angels are here on earth. You may have had a God "intervention" and know that God sent His angels to help with something in your life (like a near-death experience or miraculous event). Or maybe, like Elisha (or even myself), you can see the spiritual realm[46] and watch God's protection around you. Regardless of whether you know these created beings have helped you out, they have shaped history (with God's direction) throughout the generations.

How many of us pray "on earth as it is in Heaven"? I think we forget that angels are a part of the fullness of God's perfect Heavenly Kingdom—a place where His will is unopposed and unquestioned—24/7. I am always in awe when I think about this, as angels experience that right now. Imagine being in God's presence continuously without sin being present—just the fullness of joy and abundance of His pure, unconditional love, without satan trying to butt in.

---

[46] 2 Kings 6:17-20.

Yet, with God being Sovereign, let's remember His reverence; knowing this fact requires us to remember that He is omnipotent (all-powerful), omniscient (all-knowing), and omnipresent (all-present). In other words, He always has all power over all things and in all ways. Those are just a few of His attributes; there are many more.

As shared earlier, even though angels have been given free will (like us), the difference is that they *always* choose to follow Yahweh and His perfect commandments. This means that angels' actions can be visible to us (we can see the outcome of their actions in the natural sense) to ensure God's purpose is met. Angels do the will of their Creator, and thus, God uses them in any way He chooses.

I encourage us that when we think about angels, it allows us to think beyond the world we immediately live in and begin to understand that there are things at work that some of us may never quite comprehend. Ultimately, though, angels are here to point us towards God. Therefore, the next time you pray "on earth as it is in Heaven," understand that what you are speaking is a prophetic declaration of longing for something more than what we can see right now.

I have already spoken about some angels' sole purpose: to help humanity fulfil God's master plan for us until eternity begins. Therefore, let's focus on the angels here on earth and God's roles for them. As I discussed in an earlier chapter, we know that angels are God's messengers, but God has sent angels throughout Scripture to bring His Word to His people.

However, something even more essential to comprehend is that there is nowhere in Scripture where God asks an angel to serve or help non-Christians. Now, you might be thinking, well, what about when you were a little girl, Rebecca, and raised as an atheist? I often pondered this myself, but I found the answer within Scripture. The Bible describes angels in Hebrews 1:14 as ministering spirits sent to serve those <u>who are to</u> inherit salvation, which is the defining point. Therefore, the Bible states that this refers to those who <u>will come</u> to know Jesus as Lord and Saviour…whether at that moment or in their future; God already knows who will be with Him in Heaven when Jesus returns. Therefore, in His infinite wisdom, He directs angels to minister to us as He sees fit.

That should be the greatest comfort for us. It's not the knowledge that everything will be all right, but that everything is already under control. It is the knowledge that we have a God who is infinite in his mercies, love, and kindness. Therefore, what comforted me when walking through this journey called life was not just knowing the character of God, but more, I realised how deeply God cared for me as His daughter. Think about it…He cares for the birds in the sky… He cares for the deer in the mountains… and about the sun rising and setting and even controlling the waves and the winds… Yet, He cares more for me. This means that even though the world is chaotic. If God controls everything within the natural world and the spiritual world, then He controls all the chaos anyway; it's about trusting God that He will give us what we need when we need it.

So, back to the angels, and yes, as mentioned, they minister to us to help God's elect. So, think of when Jesus was tempted for forty days, and the angels came to Him.[47] Or when Paul experienced a visitation at sea,[48] or even Peter, when the angel helped him escape prison[49]— Angels served the people that God saves.

But they are also sent to destroy or execute judgement as well. Therefore, don't believe that angels are all happy, joy, joy. Just think of the Passover in Exodus 12:23. What about Balaam in Numbers 22. Then, the Assyrian army was slaughtered in 2 Kings 19:35 by angels. Angels will carry out God's judgement as God determines. We may struggle with this fact, but God uses angels in any way He chooses in His infinite wisdom. This means that because we know hardly anything outside of our Universe, we cannot fathom the full purposes that angels fulfil in God's master plan. We need to have a

---

[47] Matthew 4:11. [48] Acts 27:23-24. [49] Acts 12:6-10.

grateful heart that the LORD uses angels in many unseen ways for His glory and purpose.

The War Humanity Faces

We are currently in the fight of our lives, and most people are unaware. It's this beautiful impossibility of living in a holding period where we are waiting for Christ's return, and that Godly order is restored, so our eyes are fixed on Jesus. Still, we are also living in an age where the world is groaning, and we live with fear and pain all around us, as Romans 8:22-25 tells us.

So, what is happening before eternity?

There is a spiritual battle for our souls. This is a place where satan is fighting to take everyone's souls away from God, and Yahweh is battling for our unconditional love. In the arena of the world, the enemy is currently parading around like a roaring lion and masquerading as an angel of light. Both are there as a disguise to the billions of people whom he is striving to discourage, to bring false teaching upon, to cast doubt, and ultimately, for people to live without God in their lives. When a Christian stops attending church, stops praying, and even stops seeking God's will for their lives, they lessen their strength to stand up to satan.

How many of us would trust if God were to withdraw from us today? A time when we couldn't hear or even feel that He was near. Yet, we find Scriptures such as Isaiah, where he encourages us to walk in the darkness that has no light because that is where we begin to trust in the Lord, truly.[50] This is a bold step of faith that can seem like an impossible task in these last days when the world is falling apart. Still, God has given us examples from the likes of Job, where, in the "natural sense," things looked hopeless:

> *"Though he slay me, yet will I trust in Him."* Job 13:15

---

[50] Isaiah 50:10.

Submitting to God's will (even if it makes no sense) allows us to march forward even when it feels like God is firing upon us. Job had lost his family, wealth, and dignity. Yet, Job shows us that if we trust in God, He will prove that He has never stopped fighting for us and has a plan, like Esther going to speak for her people even when death was possible. Or Ruth following Naomi when all hope seemed to be fading. When we trust, God helps us realise that an unseen world is fighting for our freedom. So, what we believe are God's arrows coming directly at us are actually poised to kill the devil's lies around us.

In my first book, "*Life's Greatest Battles,*"[51] I wrote about the armour of God and how it is a weapon for Christians to use when overcoming the battles they face. As spiritual beings, we can frustratingly forget that man can only kill our physical body. Yet, it is God who can destroy both our soul and body (Matthew 10:28). So, why do we fail to put on spiritual armour each day when this spiritual battle rages on?

It's been over five years since that book was published, and over that time, it has allowed me to think about this on a deeper level. I still see firsthand, Christians struggling day by day because they forget the ABC of warfare.

For instance, when Paul talks about the armour in Ephesians 6:10-18, he describes it as Roman Armour. Yet, strip this back even more, and verse ten reveals the "why" behind the Armour of God in the first place:

> *"Finally, be strong in the Lord and in the strength of his might."*
> Ephesians 6:10

When we pray the armour over us, we are putting on Christ's strength, enabling us to overcome anything satan would throw at us. Without it, we are a child unarmed in this universal war, thus becoming easy pickings for satan. Therefore, without the armour, we are without Christ.

---

[51] Life's Greatest Battles, published by Maurice Wylie Media, 2019.

William Gurnell[52] puts it so powerfully when he states that a person in a Christless, graceless state is naked and unarmed and so unfit to fight Christ's battles against sin and satan. This is because God at first sent man forth in complete armour, 'being created in righteousness and true holiness,' but the devil stripped him, and therefore, as soon as the first sin was completed, it is written that 'they were naked.'[53h]

Christians today are spiritually naked, let alone the rest of the world. We are not praying, reading our Bibles, and having accountability from other believers, as we live in a generation that believes everything taught about the Acts church is irrelevant.

Ephesians offers us a window into the spiritual realities that underlie our struggles and difficulties. The sins we commit against God, ourselves, and others spring from a deeper well than simple bad choices or circumstances. Believers are engaged in spiritual warfare, which is why the actual fight is not with flesh and blood but with the heavenly realm.[54]

If you want more encouragement about the battle you are facing, read 2 Corinthians 10:1-6, as it offers additional teaching from Paul concerning warfare. Combining these passages shows the spiritual battle behind the scenes of many of our life experiences. Arguments we face against the Gospel, failures of Biblical morality and the vast amount of unbiblical thinking within the world… make no mistake, these aren't just our incorrect beliefs, but as Paul says, these are intentionally being brought forth by the enemy who influences the world.

The War Angels Face

I vividly remember coming out of my school classroom and looking at a spiritual battle in the sky. Everyone around me was carrying on as if nothing was happening, and yet, I sat down in the playground and just looked up in awe as the angels took on the demonic. There

---

[52] English author and preacher in 17th Century.   [53] Genesis 3:7.   [54] Ephesians 6:12.

were so many individual battles from Heaven's Army within the vast blue sky that I could see, but nowadays, I have had to learn to live in the natural sense whilst still seeing the spiritual realm and all that goes with it, but I count it as a privilege to see what I do.

When I think of people within Scripture who saw the "invisible" realm, then you have Elisha in 2 Kings 6:11-17, which I mentioned in a previous chapter, and Daniel in Daniel 10:7:17. These incredible stories represent different scenarios that were taking place around them at the time. God allowed them to bridge a gap in the physical realm to see what was happening spiritually. Then, the Lord even opened the eyes of Elisha's servant to see the host of God's army. His spiritual eyes were opened to see into the warfare around him. Whereas only Daniel saw the angel before him, everyone else felt the terror and fled from the scene. Daniel was also granted access to see, hear, and speak spiritually as he communicated with the angel.

Do we need to ask, what is happening now regarding the wage of the spiritual battle that most cannot see?

Well, God's Army is fighting the spiritual darkness sent to try to stop God's plans for saving us (think of Daniel in the passage listed above). Some people have said to me that if angels or demons can't die and they don't suffer physical wounds, what is the point of the spiritual battle? I have covered this throughout the book already, but angels go into battle to deliver messages from God,[55] but it's more than that; Scripture shows us that angels also remove the demonic from the heavenly.[56] It also shows that demons can be withstood as told in James 4:7, and even tortured by God in Luke 8:28, lose what they possess found in Mark 9:25-26. Some were sent to another place in Matthew 8:32 and were removed to the Abyss in Luke 8:31. But the reality of this battle is, that it affects everyone, whether we like it or not.

---

[55] Daniel 10:13. [56] Revelation 12:7-8.

Angel's roles in Death

I find great comfort in the fact that angels guide believers to heaven when they pass away. Death is something everyone faces and often fears, including Christians. However, in the Bible, death is portrayed not as the end of life but as a separation. Physical death separates the soul from the body, spiritual death separates us from God, and eternal death separates us from heaven. For Christians, the separation of soul and body is temporary; at the resurrection, our souls will be reunited with glorified bodies.

I have shown that angels play a significant role throughout our lives, but I want to show you that this is also part of their role in death. When Lazarus died, angels carried him to be with Abraham in heaven.[57] This aligns with the comforting thought that angels, as ministering spirits, are sent to serve those who will inherit salvation.

If angels are involved in our lives, their role becomes even more significant when our souls transition to be with our Saviour at death. If you remember, I spoke on the three heavens in an earlier chapter—our souls need to pass through the atmospheric heaven (first) and then the celestial heaven (second) on our way to the Third Heaven, where God resides. Therefore, we need the protection and guidance of angels, because if satan sends the demonic to halt Daniel from getting his prayer answered for three weeks, how much more opposition would satan bring to a soul trying to reach the Father? So, angels will escort us safely through those realms, and this is also shown when Jesus returns in glory, accompanied by His angels, who will then attend to those making their transport to heaven as our heavenly ushers.[58]

---

[57] Luke 16:22.   [58] 1 Thessalonians 4:16.

CHAPTER SIX
Unveiling God's Eternal Master Plan

"Those in whom the Spirit comes to live are God's new Temple. They are, individually and corporately, places where heaven and earth meet."

N. T. Wright (New Testament Bible Scholar)

The Bible tells an incredible story of themes, details, and characters. Still, much like a movie, this story can only be fully understood when we start at the beginning and work our way systematically towards the conclusion.

This, therefore, is the same for understanding God's "master plan," as every part of the Bible needs to be understood in the context of the one storyline, because it ultimately reveals what God has said and done within history through His divine activity for angels and humanity, showing us this one overarching story.[i]

In my early Christian days, I saw the Bible as fragmented or disconnected, even, particularly when comparing one testament to the other. I remember—and this is cringeworthy—that I even told one of my unbeliever friends in the UK that the Old Testament wasn't real; it was simply a collection of stories.

You will be pleased to know that my theology has dramatically improved. Still, every Bible passage, book, and testament is intricately connected and tells one story about God's redemptive plan to see God and humanity together once more, which is ultimately revealed through Christ.

God's master plan of Temple Living is seen from Genesis to Revelation, and I want to show you this. Still, being honest, when you think about temples, I don't think they have a very positive connotation in the 21st Century within the Western World. People often think of temples as being bound up with stuffy religious things like idols and icons, or maybe when we think of temples, it's around different religions like Buddhism or Hinduism. Yet, in the Bible, temple living must be an essential foundation in understanding God's narrative because this is the reason for it all.

Temple living explains the past, present, and future. It's the reason Jesus became flesh and died for us. It has been the plan since the beginning of time, and yet humanity has done a stellar job of mucking up this plan along the way. However, God knew that this would happen. So, He inspired sixty-six books to be written so that the Bible would show His true vision for temple living, and reveal His ultimate master plan to us, along with the angels being there every step to help fulfil this plan.

Do we need to ask, where does the Bible's story of temple living begin?

> *"In the beginning God created the heavens and the earth."*
> Genesis 1:1

It starts at the very beginning. Yet, in those ten simple words found on page one of our beautiful Bible, the story of God's plan for humanity commences, and we learn that God created a design for His creation.

This means that from Genesis 1-2, the world was as God intended. He and His creation were united. But Genesis 3 is where the problem begins—because after the "fall," we see that humanity became separated from God.

Hindsight is a great thing! We can look back and see that God designed a garden paradise where humanity would dwell with Him forever. This should have been the beginning and the end of the story, full stop.

So, what is the most important thing we need to grasp within God's master plan?

As I said, it's understanding Temple Living within Scripture, which, for us today, means being in God's presence. Genesis 3 through to Revelation 22, sets out God's beautiful plan for humanity to dwell with Him again.

The Garden Temple

When God opened this revelation to me, it changed my life, and I believe it will also change yours. Genesis 1-3 is where "temple living" is introduced as the meeting place between God and humanity. In other words, the Garden of Eden allowed humanity to experience temple living. But this was supposed to mean being in the presence of God for all of eternity, as mentioned. So, when God said to Adam and Eve to:

> *"Be fruitful and increase in number."* Genesis 1:28

As His image bearers,[59] if it weren't for sin, humanity would have seen the glory of God spread throughout the world, because the world is God's temple. Humanity was made in God's image, and yet, although humanity (for a time) was in the right standing with God, they desired to become wise like Him through satan's deception.[60]

---

[59] Genesis 1:26-27. [60] Genesis 3:1-7.

Yet, to sum this up, we know that in Genesis 3:14-15, God promised that victory would come from a descendant of the woman to one day crush the head of the serpent. Therefore, due to Adam and Eve living in the garden as God's priests, working and keeping the garden[61] and tending to this Holy space, because of sin, God had to exile them from the ordered Eden temple into the chaos of the wilderness.

Therefore, God's master plan to bring back temple living begins on this foundation found in Genesis 3:8:

> *"They heard the sound of the LORD God walking in the garden in the cool of the day."*

The literal phrase there is "God walked to and fro." This exact phrase appears again when King David comes to God, wanting him to build a temple, and the LORD says back to David:

> *"Since the day I brought Israel up from Egypt, I have been moving about in a tent for my dwelling."* 2 Samuel 7:6-7

The language God uses for His movement in the Tabernacle parallels the language God used for His movement to and fro in the garden. In addition (incredibly), the job description of Adam and Eve matches the job description of the first priests or temple servants later in the Bible. We're told:

> *"The LORD God took the man and put him in the garden to work it and keep it."* Genesis 2:15

This language is only used elsewhere in the Bible to describe the Levitical priests in the book of Numbers:

> *"The LORD spoke to Moses saying, 'Bring the tribe of Levi near... They shall keep guard over the whole congregation before the tent of meeting, as they work at the tabernacle."* Numbers 3 5-7

---

[61] Genesis 2:15; Numbers 18:1-8.

In a sense, Adam and Eve in the garden were prototypes of what would one day become the priests in the Tabernacle. We see this in how priests offered sacrifices in the temple for their sins and those of others. And so, Adam would also have his and his wife's sins atoned for through a sacrifice that would "cover" or atone for their sins by God Himself.[62]

But what happens? We know that sin enters the garden, and humanity is cast out, but who does God place at the entrance to guard the way back?

> *"After He drove the man out, He placed on the east side of the Garden of Eden cherubim and a flaming sword flashing back and forth to guard the way to the tree of life."* Genesis 3:24

The cherubim stand at the gate, because as always, these angels guard the holiness of God's presence.

The Wilderness Tabernacle

So, fast-forward a few generations, and eventually, Jacob, who is a descendant of Adam, Abraham, and Isaac, would have twelve sons, and eventually, their descendants would wind up being enslaved in Egypt. God hears the cries of His people and raises Moses to deliver Israel from their slavery through the Red Sea and into the wilderness—which you can read about in Exodus 14.

It says that Israel sojourned (which is a fancy word for "dwelt or dwelling somewhere"), but Israel as we know it was in the wilderness for much longer than they hoped for because God had judged them by prolonging their wilderness wanderings for forty years. This was because of their thankless and faithless grumbling and idolatry—which you can read about in Exodus chapters 16 and 32.

---

[62] Genesis 3:21.

But, as God did in the garden, He would not give up on dwelling with His people. God desired His glory to fill the earth, even amid sin. Think about the Garden of Eden, where God still pursued Adam and Eve in their sin, by asking:

> *"Where are you?"* Genesis 3:9

Then, in the wilderness, we see that God would still pursue His people. For forty years, the Lord initiated the building of the Tabernacle where isolated sacrifices would be offered, just like the one in the Garden of Eden, as a way to fill this dwelling with His glory throughout their journeys during their wanderings. This was God's way of reversing the curse of the fall.

As mentioned, humanity's sin meant that we could not dwell with the Holy God who made us. Our sin ultimately separated us from God's presence. But the tabernacle would be His expression, as it says in Psalm 23:6:

> *"Goodness and mercy pursuing us all the days of our lives that we might dwell in the house of the LORD forever."*

So, the tabernacle became a mobile temple, where God's presence was then among His people in the wilderness. And who shows up again? The cherubim.

> *"Make two cherubim out of hammered gold at the ends of the cover… The cherubim are to have their wings spread upward, overshadowing the cover with them. The cherubim are to face each other, looking toward the cover. There, above the cover between the two cherubim that are over the ark of the covenant law, I will meet with you…"* Exodus 25:18-22

Don't miss that: God's presence dwells between the cherubim. Remember that the Seraphim are above Him, Cherubim beside Him, and Thrones below.

The Jerusalem Temple

We find in the Book of Joshua, 400+ years later, that the Israelites had entered the promised land. It became a new kind of garden paradise—or even a new kind of temple for them. Joshua 5 shows that it is a land where God will once again dwell with His people. Here, the temple pattern is established once more. We can read that the temple is promised in 2 Samuel 7:1-16, and the dwelling was built in 1 Kings 5-8. Sadly, it was destroyed in 2 Kings 25 and rebuilt in Ezra 3. God made a covenant with King David, as told in Psalm 89:3-4, that He would establish his royal line forever. King David desired to build a house in the name of the Lord, but could not due to the warfare and his enemies surrounding him. Therefore, the LORD promised David that his son, Solomon, would build His house and reign forever and ever. This would then fulfil the promise of a permanent dwelling place for God amongst His people.[63] So, from here, the glory returns; the presence fills the house; and once again, angels are everywhere in the design. Massive cherubim carved from olive wood stand in the inner sanctuary. Angelic figures are embroidered into the curtain. The whole building shouts: This is the place of God's holy presence.

Now, I wish I could say it was good news from here, but we read that Solomon partially fulfilled this promise by building the glorious Jerusalem temple, but sadly, he would not reign forever as king. In 1 Kings 11, he plummeted himself into idolatry and sin, and his descendants would rupture the kingdom of Israel in two (1 Kings 12) by wanting to rule on their terms. The temple structure was destroyed once more in 586 BC by Nebuchadnezzar, King of Babylon.

Babylon became God's instrument of judgement toward His people by carrying them off into exile. The Babylonians burned and pillaged the city of Jerusalem, destroyed its temple, and seemingly eliminated the hope of God dwelling with His people again.

---

[63] 2 Samuel 7:12-13.

Yet, the prophets envisioned a new temple in 538 BC, which would become a place where God would again recreate His world for humanity to be His image-bearers and for the Israelites to rebuild the house of the LORD when they finally returned to Jerusalem from their exile—this was under an edict by Cyrus, King of Persia.[64]

By 515 BC, the residents who knew the glory of the first temple wept bitterly because God's presence would not gloriously manifest itself there as before, once the second Temple had been completed:

> *"so that the people could not distinguish the sound of the joyful shout from the sound of the people's weeping, for the people shouted with a great shout, and the sound was heard far away."* Ezra 3:13

This temple took over twenty years to complete and, even then, was less impressive than Solomon's, because despite its grandeur, the glory of God never returned to it in the same way as before. In other words, because God's presence was no longer dwelling there, no cherubim were guarding the Holy of Holies, which meant that there was no visible sign of His indwelling glory. And yet, it is in this very temple that angels reappear in the story of redemption: Gabriel stands before Zechariah in the temple to announce the birth of John the Baptist (Luke 1:11–13); the same angel visits Mary to proclaim that she will bear the Messiah (Luke 1:26–28); and at Christ's birth, a multitude of the heavenly host fills the skies, praising God and declaring peace on earth (Luke 2:13–14). In all of this, the angels were bearing witness to something greater—that the true temple, Jesus Christ Himself, was about to come. But before this, Malachi 2:1-9 reveals that the priests and the temple were sadly still corrupt, and this is where the Old Testament canon closes, and from this point, 400 years elapse.

---

[64] Ezra 1:2-3; 3:10-11.

Jesus Christ, the True Temple

Readers of God's temple story are led to ask whether all hope of God dwelling with His people was lost. But the ultimate fulfilment of God's promise is to dwell inseparably with His people through Jesus Christ.

In Ezekiel, he says:

> *"Although I have scattered you in the countries of the world, I will be a sanctuary to you."* Ezekiel 11:16

In that promise, the Lord identifies Himself with temple living because He promises to come and be the temple, and that promise is fulfilled in John 1:14, where John reminds us that the Word became flesh and dwelt among us.

Herod the Great (by this time) had already rebuilt and established a temple. Still, Jesus declared that the Jerusalem temple was corrupt by saying His house would be called a house of prayer—they had made the temple a den of robbers.[65] From this, we see the true and better temple built in the incarnation of Jesus Christ Himself. He is the place where God dwells with humanity. Colossians reaffirms this by saying:

> *"In him the fullness of deity dwells bodily."* Colossians 2:9

In other words, Christ Himself is the ultimate place where God is known, served, worshipped, and present.

However, it wouldn't take long for humanity to tear the temple down that Herod had built. In John 2, Jesus enters the temple and is asked for a sign. And He answers:

> *"Destroy this temple, and in three days I will raise it up… But he was speaking about the temple of his body,"* John 2:19-21

---

[65] Matthew 21:13.

We know that the crucifixion is the ultimate destruction of the temple of God. Yet, the resurrection is its rebuilding because when Jesus rose from the grave, He defeated satan and fulfilled the promise of God as told in Philippians 2:5-11. Also, in the resurrection is God's powerful message that the only true and acceptable sacrifice offered by His true and great high priest, Jesus Christ, has been accepted and approved[66]—Hallelujah! In other words, Jesus Christ, the true Temple, is promised, built, destroyed, and rebuilt, just like Solomon's temple in Jerusalem.

So where were the angels in relation to Christ, who is Himself the true temple? The fullness of God's presence dwelt in Him, and throughout His life the angels surrounded and ministered to Him. After His temptation in the wilderness, Matthew 4:11 tells us that angels came and served Him. In Gethsemane, as He agonised in prayer before the cross, Luke 22:43 records that an angel appeared and strengthened Him. At His resurrection, angels declared the triumphant words: *"He is not here; He is risen!"* (Matthew 28:6). And at the moment of His death, the temple veil was torn in two, opening the way for every believer to enter directly into God's presence through Christ.

The Church as Spiritual Temple

We are now within the Book of Acts, and because of Jesus' death and resurrection, God's Holy Spirit would become God's presence to believers, where He would dwell in them to establish the church as God's *spiritual temple.*[67]

Yet, in this new temple, God promised to be with His people, always, even to the end of the age, and this was fulfilled at Pentecost, when the Holy Spirit was poured out on Jews and Gentiles alike in Acts 2:1-4.

---

[66] Hebrews 7:23-25. [67] 1 Corinthians 6:19-20.

But, it was more than that because a new race of garden priests would be raised in this place—a people of God's own possession.[68] In other words, every Jesus Follower or even the corporate body of Christ (the Church)—even though it is currently the "imperfect meeting place"—would become the meeting place between God and sinners. And the temple, from this point on, would transform from being a building to people.

How amazing that we can enjoy God's presence in a way that King David and Solomon could never have anticipated!

Now watch this regarding the angels, as through Jesus, God's presence no longer dwells in a building of stone but in His people. We know from above that at Pentecost, the fire of heaven fell, and the Spirit filled the disciples, marking a new era where God Himself would make His home within us. Paul reminds us:

> 1 Corinthians 3:16, *"Don't you know that you yourselves are God's temple and that God's Spirit dwells in your midst?"*

And Peter echoes the same truth:

> 1 Peter 2:5, *"You also, like living stones, are being built into a spiritual house to be a holy priesthood, offering spiritual sacrifices acceptable to God through Jesus Christ."*

We are now the temple—living stones joined together into a holy dwelling for the Lord. And once again, angels are not far from this reality. In Revelation chapters 2–3, Jesus addresses each church through their angel, and Hebrews 1:14 tells us that angels are sent to minister to those who will inherit salvation—that's you and me.

---

[68] 1 Peter 2:4-5.

The New Jerusalem Temple

This leads us to the Book of Revelation, where the New Jerusalem is described as a new kind of "Holy of Holies." It promises to function as the eternal dwelling place of God with His people, as Revelation 21:3 tells us, and it will also be a new garden-city paradise where the water of life flows from the very Throne of God[69]—meaning there will be no temple structure from this point. This is where we will be forever in God's temple—His presence—where God is known, served, worshipped, and present to us.

This is where redeemed sinners, sanctified on earth, will become glorified in Christ. We will dwell forever with a Holy God because the Lamb who was slain ushers us into God's perfect temple—Himself, and this is what God's whole plan has been about: *God dwelling with His people forever.* The temple is not a building anymore. The temple is God Himself, with us, and us with Him.

From Eden to the New Jerusalem, the story has always been the same: God wanting to dwell with us, and Angels serve this plan, and will continue to do so until Jesus returns. They guard; they worship; they fight; and they announce. But the centre of it all is not the angels — it's Jesus. So, let's live aware. Let's live aligned. Let's live anticipating His return, because the day is coming when the dwelling of God will be with His people, and we will see the Father, face to face.

And so, finally, as I close, I pray that the hope God has given us with the angels and His master plan has been revealed to you as you have read this book.

We have incredible joy to look forward to seeing this final perfect temple come to fulfilment as the LORD God Almighty and the Lamb Himself.[70]

---

[69] Revelation 22:3.   [70] Revelation 21:22.

Yet, what I love is that God will wipe away every tear from our eyes as the realisation comes to us all that death has finally been defeated. There will be no more crying, no more pain, no more separation from our Heavenly Father; just temple living—forever—as we were initially intended to be, with God the Father, God the Son and God the Holy Spirit and the angels.

Notes

Chapter One

a) *Matthew 1:20–21, Matthew 2:13, Matthew 2:19–20, Matthew 4:11, Matthew 28:2–7, Luke 1:11–20, Luke 1:26–38, Luke 2:8–14, Luke 22:43, John 20:12, Acts 1:10–11, Acts 5:19, Acts 8:26, Acts 10:3–7, Acts 12:7–11, Acts 27:23–24, Revelation 1:1, Revelation 5:2–5, Revelation 7:13–14, Revelation 10:8–10, Revelation 17:1–3, Revelation 19:9–10, Revelation 21:9–10, Revelation 22:8–9, Hebrews 1:14, Hebrews 13:2, Galatians 1:8, 1 Corinthians 11:10, 1 Thessalonians 4:16.*

Chapter Two

b) "What Does It Mean For The Saints To Judge Angels?" Kyle Dillon. The Gospel Coalition, https://www.thegospelcoalition.org/article/saints-judge-angels/.
c) "Intro to Spiritual Beings." Bible Project, *https://bibleproject.com/explore/video/intro-spiritual-beings/*
d) *"Angel of the Lord."* Bible Project, https://bibleproject.com/explore/video/angel-lord/#fn-4

Chapter Three

e) Graham Billy. *Angels: God's Secret Agents.* (Nashville, TN: Thomas Nelson, 1975), 57.
f) "The Nine Choirs of Angels." Catholic Online, *https://www.catholic.org/saints/angels/angelchoir.php*

Chapter Four

g) *"What are the Three Heavens."* Don Stewart. Blue Letter Bible, https://www.blueletterbible.org/faq/don_stewart/don_stewart_151.cfm.

Chapter Five

h) Gurnall William. *"The Christian in Complete Armour."* (Peabody, BOS: Hendrickson Publishers, 2014), 45-46

Chapter Six

i) Craig G. Bartholomew and Michael W. Goheen, *The Drama of Scripture: Finding Our Place in the Biblical Story.* 2nd Edition (UK: SPCK Publishing, 2014), 14.

To Contact the Author

www.RebeccaBrand.org

 @rebeccabrand.page

 @rebecca.brand

Inspired to write a book?

Contact

Maurice Wylie Media
Your Inspirational & Christian Book Publisher
Based in Northern Ireland and distributing around the world

www.MauriceWylieMedia.com

www.ingramcontent.com/pod-product-compliance
Lightning Source LLC
Chambersburg PA
CBHW061222070526
44584CB00029B/3945